Refusing War, Affirming Peace

Refusing War, Affirming Peace

A HISTORY OF CIVILIAN PUBLIC SERVICE CAMP #21 AT CASCADE LOCKS

Jeffrey Kovac

foreword by Paul S. Boyer

Oregon State University Press • Corvallis

Cover photograph: Worker at Cascade Locks, c. 1942. Photographer probably Henry Dasenbrock. Schrock Collection, image 38. Lewis & Clark College Special Collections, Portland, OR.

The paper in this book meets the guidelines for permanence and durability of the Committee on Production Guidelines for Book Longevity of the Council on Library Resources and the minimum requirements of the American National Standard for Permanence of Paper for Printed Library Materials Z39.48-1984.

Library of Congress Cataloging-in-Publication Data
Kovac, Jeffrey.
 Refusing war, affirming peace : a history of Civilian Public Service Camp #21 at Cascade Locks / Jeffrey Kovac; foreword by Paul S. Boyer.
     p. cm.
 Includes bibliographical references and index.
 ISBN 978-0-87071-575-4 (alk. paper)
 1. Civilian Public Service. Camp #21 (Cascade Locks, Or.) 2. World War, 1939-1945--Conscientious objectors — Oregon — Cascade Locks. 3. Conscientious objectors — Oregon — Cascade Locks — History — 20th century. 4. Church of the Brethren--Oregon--Cascade Locks — History — 20th century. 5. World War, 1939-1945 — Oregon — Cascade Locks. 6. Cascade Locks (Or.) — History — 20th century. 7. Cascade Locks (Or.) — Social life and customs — 20th century. 8. Cascade Locks (Or.) — Social conditions — 20th century. I. Title.
 D810.C82K68 2009
 940.53'1620973--dc22

2009012968

Oregon State University Press
121 The Valley Library
Corvallis OR 97331-4501
541-737-3166 • fax 541-737-3170
http://oregonstate.edu/dept/press

For Susan

CONTENTS

Foreword

"Pacifism . . . is not a matter of calm[ly] looking on; it is work, hard work."

Käthe Kollwitz, February 21, 1944

Amid the torrent of books recalling America's World War II experience on the battlefield and the home front, one facet of that experience has received scant attention. This is the history of a small but significant number of Americans who for reasons of conscience refused military service despite massive pressure to fight in what has come to be called "the good war." Many of these young men belonged to one of the so-called "historic peace churches:" the Society of Friends (Quakers); the Church of the Brethren; and the various branches and offshoots of the Mennonites, including the Amish and the Brethren in Christ, the denomination in which I was reared. Heirs to pacifist beliefs stretching back through the centuries to the very beginnings of Christianity, these groups preached non-resistance and encouraged young men of draft age to honor the Bible's injunctions against violence and killing, even if it meant refusing their government's demand to take up arms in time of war.

In World War I, an earlier generation of conscientious objectors (COs) faced only two stark choices: prison or non-combatant service in the military. In World War II, however, thanks to the efforts of leaders from the historic peace churches, the government provided an alternative: performing work in the national interest in a non-military program called Civilian Public Service (CPS) for the war's duration and six months beyond. Some twelve thousand young COs, mostly from the peace churches, but also Catholics, Jehovah's Witnesses, members of various mainstream Protestant denominations, and some with no religious affiliation at all, chose the CPS option. While some worked in mental hospitals, in medical-experimentation programs, or other individual or small-group assignments, most were sent to remote camps in wilderness or semi-wilderness areas where they engaged in forestry work, soil conservation, trail maintenance, fire fighting, and similar outdoor tasks. The New Deal's Civilian Conservation Corps

8

(CCC) for jobless youth in the 1930s provided the model for CPS. Indeed, many CPS camps had formerly been CCC facilities.

Mostly out of the public eye at the time, and only dimly remembered today, the CPS program profoundly influenced the young men who served in it, along with their families and loved ones. Often having little in common with their camp-mates apart from a shared objection to military service, CPS men found themselves interacting with others of differing cultural backgrounds, religious beliefs, and political orientation, ranging from quietist withdrawal to radical activism. The CPS experience also fostered personal skills and talents — manual, verbal, aesthetic, and intellectual — that in some cases prepared the way for future careers in the arts, academia, politics, business, and public service. For example, one young man at Oregon's Cascade Locks camp, Wendell Harmon, gained experience as editor of the camp newsletter that later stood him in good stead in writing a Ph.D. dissertation in American history at UCLA and as a college history professor.

The Civilian Public Service program has attracted historians' attention, including its role as a prototype for the later Peace Corps and other national-service programs. And CPS, of course, figures in general histories of pacifism in America and studies of the draft and of the government's handling of conscientious objectors throughout U.S. history. Yet we have very few micro-level accounts of the actual experience of individuals in specific camps. Jeffrey Kovac's history of the CPS camp sponsored by the Church of the Brethren at Cascade Locks, Oregon, is thus especially welcome. Initially drawn to the story by conversations with his father-in-law, a World War II CO who served at Cascade Locks, Kovac went on to mine a rich array of primary sources, including letters, ephemeral documents, reunion videotapes, and oral-history interviews. From this research he has crafted an engaging and illuminating close-up account of life in a CPS camp. A professor of chemistry at the University of Tennessee, he clearly also possesses a knack for historical investigation and writing.

The choice of Cascade Locks — situated some forty miles east of Portland in the beautiful Columbia River valley near Mount Hood — is a particular happy one. Not only was this the largest CPS camp, but it brought together an unusually diverse and talented group of COs with interests in literature, architecture, music, politics, philosophy, religion, and the arts. In addition, its director Mark Schrock, a young Church of the Brethren minister from Indiana, possessed an exceptional knack for community building and nurturing the leadership potential and varied talents of the camp residents. Further, Cascade Locks gained national attention when America's best-known CO, the film actor Lew Ayres, was assigned there.

Far from sitting out the war in wilderness isolation and repetitive, mind-numbing physical labor, camp residents vigorously addressed the public issues of the day. They engaged in endless discussions; mounted a protest when the government tried to reassign one of their number, George Yamada, to a Japanese-American internment camp; resisted an assignment that some believed furthered the war effort; circulated petitions against the 1945 atomic bombing of Japan and the government's proposals for universal military training in peacetime; and pioneered postwar relief efforts in war-ravaged Europe, including sending cattle to replenish depleted herds.

On the cultural front, the young men at Cascade Locks formed reading groups; gave concerts; mounted art exhibits; published a literary magazine (one issue of which ran afoul of the postal obscenity laws!); heard lectures on timely public topics; and staged musicals and dramas, including Chekhov's *The Seagull* and a parody version of Gilbert and Sullivan's *Mikado* lampooning CPS and Selective Service officials. They painstakingly built and maintained a library of several thousand volumes (and rebuilt and restocked it after a devastating fire).

Cascade Locks even organized a "School of Pacifist Living" where, after eight hours of exhausting manual labor, participants gathered to debate the larger social and political implications of their commitment to non-violence. Some idealistic residents, including director Mark Schrock, even envisioned CPS as a utopian experiment with broad national significance. They dreamed of creating at Cascade Locks an alternative community committed to justice and democracy, nurturing the arts and the life of the mind, and embracing principles of non-violence and peaceful conflict resolution that could provide a model for the larger society when the war ended. One is reminded of other such idealistic ventures in American history, including Brook Farm, the short-lived but historically noteworthy utopian community near Boston that attracted some of New England's leading writers, intellectuals, and reformers in the 1840s.

Jeffrey Kovac's book illuminates the mundane and the quotidian as well as the exceptional. His work allows us vicariously to experience in a close-up way the day-to-day reality of life in a CPS camp, with its fatigue, frustrations, boredom, and conflicts, enlivened by moments of light-hearted diversion, passionate engagement, and genuine camaraderie that residents would fondly recall decades later.

No matter how one views the agonizing dilemmas that can arise when ethical principles clash with the demands of the state, one can surely relate on a human level to these exceptional young men who spent the war years in a CPS camp in a distant corner of the Pacific Northwest. *Refusing War, Affirming Peace* not only fleshes out a fascinating chapter in Oregon's history and illuminates a neglected facet of the nation's World War II experience, but also, in all its concrete specificity, explores issues that must continue to engage every citizen concerned with the ongoing effort to achieve a more peaceful, humane, cultivated, and authentically democratic American society—goals so often invoked rhetorically and so rarely achieved in practice.

Paul Boyer
Merle Curti Professor of History Emeritus
University of Wisconsin-Madison

Acknowledgments

No book is written in isolation, and I want to thank those who have helped along the way. In my first serious venture into historical scholarship I have learned the importance of good archivists, and have had the pleasure of working with several. The records of CPS #21 are preserved at the Brethren Historical Library and Archives in Elgin, Illinois, where Kenneth Shafer and Logan Condon have made my two visits there both pleasant and productive. Doug Erickson and Paul Merchant of the Archives and Special Collections in the Aubrey R. Watzek Library at Lewis & Clark College in Portland, Oregon, have been gracious hosts during my visits to that collection. Finally, Dale F. Harter, the archivist at the Alexander Mack Memorial Library at Bridgewater College, provided access to the materials collected there.

Portions of Chapter Four were previously published as "Confrontation at the Locks," by Charles Davis and Jeffrey Kovac, in the Winter 2006 issue of the *Oregon Historical Quarterly* (Volume 107, Number 4, pp. 486-509) and are used here by permission. Permission to reproduce photographs has been given by the Archives and Special Collections at Lewis & Clark College and the Brethren Historical Library and Archives. Thanks to Jeremy Skinner at Lewis & Clark for providing digital images of the photographs from that collection. The remaining photos and other illustrations came from the collections of Julian Schrock and Charles Davis.

This book would not have been possible without the cooperation of the men of CPS #21 and their families who shared their memories and documents with me. These include Les Abbenhouse, Richard Anderson, Don Baker, Harold (Ike) Bock, Arthur Butler, Eleanor Ring Davis, Dwight Hanawalt, Wendell Harmon, Mae Rolle Henderson, Harland Gibson, Joe Gunterman, Vic Langford, Bob McLane and Sanford Rothman. Joe and Emmy Gunterman and the McLane family (Bob, Naomi, Erica and Jeff) were gracious hosts during a visit to California in the summer of 2007. The time spent with them has enriched this book. Both Richard Anderson and Joe Gunterman have read and commented on the manuscript as it has evolved.

I am particularly grateful to Julian Schrock, son of Mark Schrock, and to Don Elton Smith. Julian sent me a copy of his unpublished memoir of his family's time at Cascade Locks along with hundreds of pages of letters and other documents. He has read parts of this manuscript and answered many questions by e-mail. Not only did Don Elton Smith send me his CPS #21 files, we have maintained an active and productive correspondence since the early days of this project. He has read and made thoughtful comments on more drafts of parts of this book than I can remember, and spent most of a day in his house in Loveland, CO, patiently answering my questions and telling me stories about his experiences. One of the side benefits of this project has been getting to know Don Smith.

Many people have contributed by reading various drafts of chapters as the work progressed. These include Charles Biggs, Rev. Gordon Gibson, Jason Johnson, Roger Jones, Marianne Keddington-Lang, Rachel Kovac, and Steven Longenecker. I owe special thanks to my colleague and friend, Dan Bing, for reading a nearly final version and providing a detailed critique. As always, Donna Walter Sherwood's copyediting skills improved the flow of my prose.

I am honored that Paul S. Boyer, Merle Curti Professor of History, Emeritus, at the University of Wisconsin-Madison and a fellow conscientious objector, agreed to write a foreword for this book.

It was Paul Merchant who first encouraged me to consider writing a history of Cascade Locks. His enthusiastic support and superb copy editing skills have been essential to the success of this project.

Working with the staff of the Oregon State University Press, Mary Braun, Jo Alexander, and Tom Booth, to turn my original manuscript into an attractive published volume has been a pleasure.

I am delighted finally to have the opportunity publicly to thank James B. Barlow, my American history teacher at Sunset High School in Beaverton, Oregon, who first taught me to love history and to think critically about it.

The stories and papers of my late father-in-law, Charles Davis, stimulated my research on CPS #21, and his wisdom and humor have influenced every paragraph. I trust that he would think that writing this book was "doing the Lord's work."

Finally, and most important, the contributions of my wife, Susan Davis Kovac, to this book, and so much else, are greater than words can express. This book is dedicated to her.

CHAPTER ONE

Introduction

World War II occupies a unique space in American memory. It is the "good war" in which the "greatest generation" mobilized to defeat fascism in Europe and the Japanese in the Pacific. Through the mists of nostalgia, those years are remembered as a time of simple, old-fashioned patriotism in which the citizenry, both at home and abroad, endured tremendous sacrifice for a common cause.

As with all history, the real story is more complicated. To raise a military force of more than ten million, the U. S. Congress passed a conscription law in 1940, the Burke-Wadsworth bill, which was the first peacetime draft law in American history. Contrary to recent myth, although many volunteered or accepted conscription as their duty, the draft was not universally popular; American men did not enthusiastically embrace conscription. Those who could claim a deferment tried their best to get one, and because the decisions were made by local draft boards, their distribution mirrored the patterns of power and privilege in the country. For example, in 1942, pressure from the farm bloc resulted in the Tydings Amendment, which effectively excluded all agricultural workers from the draft.[1] But even those who did not serve in the military overwhelmingly supported the war effort, taking the good-paying jobs in the industrial machine that tooled up to produce armaments and supplies for the allied forces and buying war bonds.

A few men and women, however, refused to be a part of the war. As a country built on the principles of religious and personal freedom, the United States has always been a haven for dissenters, including those opposed to war for religious, moral or political reasons. Some of the earliest settlers of the country were Quakers, members of the Society of Friends, who have historically maintained a strong peace testimony. Other pacifist denominations, the Mennonites and Brethren, also migrated to the United States in search of religious tolerance and to avoid conscription into European armies. Pacifists and conscientious objectors (COs) have always had an uneasy relationship with the country during times of war, but the introduction of universal conscription in World War I became what Peter Brock and Nigel Young term "the harsh midwife of twentieth-century pacifism."[2] The restrictive conscription act passed by the United States Congress in 1917 gave COs only two alternatives: non-combatant service in the military, or prison. As a result, many COs were badly treated. To prevent a similar situation in World War II, the three denominations worked together to convince Congress to add to the Burke-Wadsworth Act a more liberal provision recognizing conscientious objection, which allowed for alternative service under civilian control as well as non-combatant service in the military. This history is recounted in the second chapter.

More than fifty thousand Americans chose not to fight in World War II. They fall into three broad categories. At least twenty-five thousand men accepted induction into the armed services, but requested classification as non-combatants, termed 1-A-O. They served, sometimes heroically, as medics or chaplains' assistants, or in other support roles where they were not required to bear arms. A second group, about six thousand men, refused to cooperate with the conscription law in one way or another and were sentenced to prison terms. Finally, twelve thousand men took advantage of the provision of the law that allowed them to perform alternative service, "work of national importance under civilian direction," in the program known as Civilian Public Service (CPS), a series of work camps and other projects administered primarily by the three historic peace churches (Brethren, Friends and Mennonites) under the guidance of Selective Service. These were the men classified 4-E. The first men entered CPS in 1940 expecting to spend a year in the program. After the United States entered the war, the term of service became the duration of the war plus six months, so some served for as much as four years. The last men left the CPS system in 1947.[3]

Their story, however, is little known. Shortly after the war, two of the church groups, the Brethren and Mennonites, published histories of their own projects: a projected history of the Quaker camps was never written.[4] A comprehensive study of conscientious objectors by Mulford Q. Sibley and Philip Jacob appeared in 1952.[5] In 1976 Theodore R. Wachs wrote a Ph.D. dissertation on CPS that took advantage of the extensive diary of Paul Comly French, the Executive Secretary of the National Service Board for Religious Objectors (NSBRO), the principal liaison between Selective Service and the historic peace churches.[6] A comprehensive reevaluation of the CPS system was more recently undertaken by Mitchell Lee Robinson in his doctoral dissertation.[7] Both of these valuable works unfortunately remain unpublished. Albert N. Keim wrote a brief, illustrated history that gives a nice overview of the entire CPS program.[8] Some of the individual projects, such as the work of CPS men in mental hospitals,[9] the starvation experiment,[10] and the smoke jumper unit[11] have recently received attention. A few COs have written memoirs[12] and several oral history projects have collected individual stories.[13] Richard C. Anderson, also a CO, published a study of the motivations and subsequent careers of CPS men based on an extensive survey.[14] Rachel Goossen looked at the experiences of women with significant relationships to conscientious objectors.[15] Finally, PBS produced a one-hour documentary on World War II COs along with an extensive website that includes a transcript of the broadcast.[16]

What is largely missing from the literature on CPS is a history of the camps. The camps, where the men lived and worked, were the building blocks of the program, but most writers have either looked at CPS more broadly or at the level of the individual. For example, the two most extensive studies of CPS by Sibley and Jacob and by Robinson are primarily concerned with broad issues related to conscription and alternative service. They discuss the relationship between NSBRO and Selective Service, the debates in Congress and the Roosevelt administration about CPS, and the overall administration of the program, using selected events at individual camps as illustrations. Leslie Eisan provides an excellent overview of Brethren CPS, but because his purpose is to describe and evaluate the national program, he selects appropriate examples from the various camps so the uniqueness of any individual camp is lost in the bigger picture. Individual memoirs and oral histories reveal some aspects of camp life, but in a limited way. The camp as a community has largely been ignored.

Most CPS men were assigned to what were called base camps where they lived together and worked on projects for the Departments of Interior or Agriculture, largely in forestry or soil conservation. Others were assigned to special projects, such as work in mental hospitals, where they usually lived in communal situations. The base camps were communities of fifty to two hundred men and the experiences of living together with other COs were often life-transforming. After all, these were young men, most between eighteen and twenty-six, just starting adult life, who were thrown together into a communal living situation with a diverse group of other men from all over the country. You might find a farm boy with a grade school education bunking next to a Harvard Ph.D. or a conservative Mennonite from Kansas on a work crew with an atheist socialist from New York City. Much has been written about the effect of the World War II draft on American society, how service in the military changed attitudes and paved the way for the transformation of our society. CPS was a similar experience.

Steve Cary, who was director of the Quaker CPS camp at Big Flats, New York, and later president of Haverford College, gives a good description of what was unique about life in CPS:

> *If you are in something for four years, you haven't got any money, all you can do is argue, and we would discuss every possible angle. Sometimes we would argue about Hitler, sometimes we would argue about whether we should put a lock on the refrigerator. What do you do when somebody's going to rape your grandmother? These kind of questions come up all the time.*
>
> *And out of that crucible came people who really knew why they were pacifists.*[17]

Don Elton Smith has similar things to say about Cascade Locks where he was assigned for two and a half years:

> *There was a lot of discussion among us about the tragic results of war, and of violence more generally, both physical and psychological. . . . These sorts of discussions were endless. Whenever two or three were gathered together the bull sessions would begin. We got to know each other very well. Our thinking was criticized from every angle — and I am sure it sharpened us immeasurably. No one could hide. We knew each other's weaknesses, and his strengths. No, we did not give a lot of attention to the fighting of the war, but we were continually engaged with a bigger picture of human society, searching for avenues to relieve human suffering, increase mutual understanding, and find paths to a world without war.*[18]

When they entered CPS the only thing the men had in common was that they had refused to serve in the military, but they managed to create unusual communities. The goal of this book is to understand how this happened in one particular camp: CPS #21 at Cascade Locks, Oregon.

The only published studies of individual camps are an article by Edward Orser on CPS #3 at Patapsco State Park, which discusses the building of an unintentional community[19] and Gordon Zahn's book on the short-lived Catholic CPS camp in New Hampshire known as Camp Simon. Camp Simon was first located at Stoddard, New Hampshire, (CPS #15), but was later moved to Warner, New Hampshire, where it received a new number (CPS #54).[20] Underfunded and poorly managed, Camp Simon was eventually closed by Selective Service and the men transferred to other sites. In this memoir, which is harshly critical of the CPS system, Zahn provides a striking portrait of what seems to have been a dysfunctional community, and gives voice to many of the frustrations of men in CPS: the grim reality of conscription, the meaningless work, and the lack of pay. Because of its small size, short life, and Catholic identity, Camp Simon is hardly representative of the CPS experience. Catholics comprised only about one percent of the CPS population (149 out of twelve thousand)[21] and the sponsoring agency, the Association of Catholic Conscientious Objectors (ACCO), operated only three of the approximately 150 sites: Camp Simon and two small hospital projects.[22]

In contrast, CPS Camp #21 at Cascade Locks, Oregon, was, in the words of W. Harold Row, director of Civilian Public Service for the Brethren Service Committee, "one of our most significant camps."[23] Howard Hamilton, assistant director of the camp in its last months, called it the "Athens of CPS."[24] Managed by the Church of the Brethren, CPS #21 was one of the largest and longest operating camps. Under the directorship of the Reverend Mark Y. Schrock, a Church of the Brethren minister, the camp at Cascade Locks became a vibrant community in which the men were able to pursue significant intellectual and artistic projects, including publishing a literary magazine. In 1942 the camp became nationally known when the most famous CO of World War II, the film actor Lew Ayres, arrived for a brief stay before entering the army as a medic. The men at Cascade Locks challenged Selective Service in two major protests: first concerning the relocation of a Japanese-American CO, George Yamada, and then with their refusal to participate in what they regarded as a war-related work project. The diverse population of CPS #21 included some remarkable men such as George Brown, who eventually served eighteen terms in Congress, Kermit Sheets, an important figure in the San Francisco renaissance, Kemper Nomland, a sought-after architect in Southern California, Windsor Utley, an award-winning Northwest artist, James (Jim) Townsend, a lyrical writer who went on to earn a Ph.D. in literature, and Charles (Charlie) Davis, an important public citizen in Oregon.

One of the reasons for this diversity was that Cascade Locks was operated by the Church of the Brethren.

The original informal agreement between the three historic peace churches and Selective Service was that the churches would administer and finance the camps. This seemed reasonable because it was assumed that essentially all of the COs would be members of one of the three denominations and each would take care of its own men: Mennonites would reside in Mennonite camps, Brethren in Brethren camps and Quakers in Quaker camps. This assumption proved to be false; about forty percent of the CPS population came from another, or no, denomination. Mennonites were the largest group, a bit less than forty percent of the total, and they primarily chose to be in Mennonite camps, which had the most homogeneous populations in the system. Almost everyone else went to either Brethren or Quaker camps, so these camps were both religiously and culturally diverse. The history of Cascade Locks shows how one camp successfully dealt with the problems sometimes raised by this diversity.

Theodore G. Grimsrud's ethical analysis of the World War II COs provides a good framework for understanding the various perspectives and attitudes found in CPS camps.[25] As Grimsrud points out, the standard view of the conscientious objector is that he is an independent individual responding to the dictates of conscience, a personal rejection of war: "The CO is a heroic individual who exerts his independence from social ties and champions deviant values with the strength of his will." [26] (Because the draft laws have only applied to men, Grimsrud and most other writers on this subject use gender-specific language.) This account, however, does not really describe the Mennonites, who largely became COs because of the expectations of their churches and communities. Grimsrud, a committed Mennonite, studied the CPS population as a whole, primarily through reading camp newspapers, memoirs, and conducting personal interviews, and identified what he calls four "tendencies" that describe the basic responses of COs to conscription and CPS. These four tendencies are the "resisters," the COs who rejected cooperation with the warring state, the "transformers," who were generally willing to cooperate with CPS to achieve positive social goals, the "servants," many of the Mennonites and some Brethren, who accepted the state's right to conscript and willingly cooperated with CPS, and the "separatists," primarily Jehovah's Witnesses, who had a hostile attitude toward the state and its interference with their evangelism. These tendencies, of course, are broad generalizations that can obscure the diversity of the CPS population, but they provide a useful analytic framework for understanding certain incidents in the history of CPS #21.

At the extreme, since both the "resisters" and the "separatists" rejected the compromises of CPS; most of them ended up in prison. Some rejected conscription from the outset; others started in CPS, but eventually "walked out" and were sentenced to prison terms of varying lengths. "Transformers," many of whom were inspired by the Social Gospel, viewed CPS as a way to create a more peaceful world after the war. The Social Gospel, which was founded by the American minister Walter Rauschenbusch, was the doctrine that human society could be transformed through human effort so that it approximated the Kingdom of God.[27] "Transformers" sought ways to be more useful to society and often volunteered for work in mental hospitals, medical experiments, and other detached service projects. Most "transformers" came from the mainline Protestant denominations, Methodist, Presbyterian, Episcopal, Congregational, Northern Baptists, and Disciples of Christ, but some Brethren and Mennonites also fit into this tendency. "Servants," on the other hand, were willing to accept whatever work assigned them and considered it a privilege to be allowed to serve their country. This is the classic non-resistant position of the Mennonites and related denominations, that they should obey the state as long as that obedience did not violate individual conscience. If the state wanted to wage war, that was the state's business as long as the "servant" was allowed to opt out of direct participation. "Servants" often evoked the concept of the "second mile," from the biblical injunction that if Christians are compelled to walk one mile, they should walk a second voluntarily. Although the "servants" may not have thought of CPS as ideal, most of them regarded it as the best possible option.

CPS was an imperfect system, hastily conceived and then continually revised as problems arose. Although the major policy issues surrounding CPS have been discussed at length by both Sibley and Jacob[28] and Robinson,[29] the story of Cascade Locks shows how those issues and others were confronted daily by those living in and administering a camp. The problems ranged from mundane matters such as preparing meals and doing laundry for two hundred men to moral and policy questions such as whether the work projects were too closely related to the war effort. The camps were also asked to provide appropriate educational programs and meet the religious needs of the assignees. With a population that ranged from men with a fourth grade education to some with advanced degrees, all of whom were engaged in eight or more hours of physical labor each day, crafting interesting courses required some creativity.

The history of CPS #21 is unusually well documented. Not only have the camp records been preserved, but the camp newspaper, *The Columbian,* provides a detailed picture of the first year's activities.[30] The camp records include an extensive collection of a later internal publication, *The Side Camp Newsletter,* that documents many of the activities. In 1945, the camp historian, Don Elton Smith, compiled a series of reports concerning camp activities along with autobiographies of ten assignees.[31] Both Don Elton Smith and J. Henry Dasenbrock have written personal memoirs, and Julian Schrock, son of the first camp director, has written an informal history of the time his family spent in the camp.[32] Copies of other publications, including the literary magazine *The Illiterati,* have been preserved.[33] Finally, there are two collections of video interviews with the men of CPS #21 and their wives. At the 1984 reunion organized by Charlie Davis, Norm Smith videotaped a series of group interviews along with some of the public events, a total of eight videocassettes.[34] Dave Wershkul filmed another set of interviews with COs from both Cascade Locks and the camp at Waldport, Oregon, CPS #56.[35]

There is also a personal connection. My late father-in-law, Charlie Davis, was an important figure in the history of CPS #21, so I have heard stories about the camp for more than thirty years. His personal files, which include a large number of letters, have been a rich source of information. Through Davis, I have made connections with several men from CPS #21 who have been generous in sharing both documents and memories.

As a conscientious objector myself, I have been captivated by the story of this camp. Unlike the Vietnam era when it was my turn to make a decision between peace and war, the World War II COs faced an environment that was hostile to their position. Those who sought and received the 4-E classification were a remarkable group. Many of them entered CPS with the goal of creating the core of a new pacifist society. Faced with the challenges of conscription, isolation, and physically demanding and mostly meaningless work, the men at Cascade Locks responded creatively, building a community that facilitated individual and group educational and artistic efforts. When confronted with challenges to their deeply held principles, they were willing to stand up to authority. After the war, many continued to live out the values that brought them to the camp in the first place in both their careers and in their private lives.

As I write, more than sixty years after the last CPS camp closed, it seems especially important to tell the story of those who chose peace, to honor their memory and to inspire future generations to make that same choice. The way of peace is difficult, particularly in times of war when the nation closes ranks against a common enemy. But, as World War II showed so clearly, modern warfare not only pits army against army, it also pits whole nations against whole nations. No one is immune. As Clausewitz wrote, modern war has become "an act of violence pushed to its utmost bounds."[36] With the advent of nuclear weapons, the utmost bound might well be the destruction of civilization. The story of the men of CPS and other conscientious objectors needs to be told because it shows another, more hopeful way.

CHAPTER TWO
Origins of CPS

To understand the origins of CPS it is essential to begin in 1917, the year the United States entered World War I and passed a universal conscription act, because the experiences of conscientious objectors during that war shaped the attitudes of the men who developed and administered the program, both church leaders and military leaders. The American entry into World War I found the Historic Peace Churches—Brethren, Friends (Quakers) and Mennonites—unprepared to deal with the issue of conscription. When the war broke out in 1914, United States foreign policy was isolationist, and public sentiment strongly favored neutrality in the European conflict. Public opinion and government policy began to change after the *Lusitania* sinking in May 1915, although Woodrow Wilson was reelected in 1916 with a campaign based on the slogan "He kept us out of war." Germany's announcement of unrestricted submarine warfare around the European and British coasts eventually led to a declaration of war by the United States on April 6, 1917. To build up the armed forces, a conscription law was passed on May 18, 1917.

Although several groups and influential individuals argued strenuously for more liberal treatment of conscientious objectors, the actual provision was rather narrow. Section 4 of the conscription act read:

> *Nothing in this act contained shall be construed to require or compel any person to serve in any of the forces herein provided for who is found to be a member of any well recognized religious sect or organization at present organized and existing and whose existing creed or principles forbid its members to participate in war in any form and whose religious convictions are against war or participation therein in accordance with the creed or principles of said religious organizations, but no person so exempted shall be exempted from service in any capacity that the President shall declare to be noncombatant.*

The system was set up such that anyone selected for service by a local selective service board who met the military standards was immediately inducted into the Army, whether he was a conscientious objector or not. Those who objected to both combatant and noncombatant service in the military had two alternatives. They could either refuse to register for the draft or they could register, apply for CO status, and then refuse to serve in the only option allowed by the law — noncombatant service in the military. Refusing to register meant a prison sentence; the penalty for the second alternative depended on what the military decided. Even those willing to accept noncombatant service had problems, because it took President Wilson ten months to designate the branches of the service that should be regarded as noncombatant. In an executive order dated March 20, 1918, the president declared service in the Medical Corps, the Quartermaster Corps and the Engineer Service as noncombatant. Those who refused service in those units were subject to military discipline: court martial and prison.[1]

Most COs in World War I were treated badly. Those who entered the military were subjected to enormous pressure to take up arms rather than serve in a noncombatant role and many succumbed to that pressure. Those who refused non-combatant service generally ended up in a military prison. After considerable lobbying by the peace churches Congress finally passed the Farm Furlough Act, which allowed COs to be assigned to civilian work, although still under military supervision. Most were furloughed for farm work, although some men went to Europe to work for the American Friends Service Committee.

The usual prison term for absolutist COs, those who were unwilling to cooperate with any system of conscription and therefore refused both combatant and non-combatant service, was twenty to twenty-five years. Some received life sentences, and seventeen were given death sentences. None of the death sentences was carried out, and most of the more severe prison sentences were modified on review. No CO, however, actually served more than three years in prison; the last were pardoned and released in November 1920. Prison life was brutal in both civilian and military prisons. COs were characterized as unpatriotic cowards. Some were tortured and two Hutterites, the Hofer brothers, died in prison as a result of mistreatment. Eventually work strikes and other protests by COs convinced the War Department to make the worst forms of brutality such as manacling men to cell bars illegal for military prisoners.[2]

Neither the government nor the military ever came to a satisfactory resolution of the problem of conscientious objection during World War I. The administration wanted to keep the number of conscientious objectors at a minimum. Caught up in the war hysteria, no one in authority seemed able to understand that COs were sincere in their convictions. In the words of Rufus Jones, Quaker philosopher, theologian and long-time Haverford College professor, and an important figure in working with the government to obtain better treatment for COs during this period, "It apparently did not occur to the Washington people that our objection was anything more than an objection to the direct killing of people. They do not seem to understand that we are opposed to the military system and all forms of service under that system. I find it difficult to make anybody in Washington realize that attitude."[3]

The experience of World War I stimulated the three denominations, Brethren, Friends and Mennonites, to work together in the postwar period although theological differences made cooperation difficult. Several conferences were held beginning in 1923, which led to the formation of a joint committee of the three denominations in 1936 to coordinate their peace efforts. This cooperation paved the way for the successful effort to provide better alternatives for COs in World War II, in particular the system of alternative service that became known as Civilian Public Service (CPS).

The CPS system had its direct origin in a visit to President Franklin D. Roosevelt by seven representatives of the Historic Peace Churches on January 10, 1940. Even though the war in Europe was in its early stages, the United States was rapidly moving into a prewar preparation phase. At that meeting the church representatives presented the president with a letter and expressed their concern that should war come, adequate provision be made for conscience. They proposed a system of alternative civilian service and complete exemption for absolutists. Their proposals were modeled on the liberal and successful system for conscientious objectors in Great Britain. The president was quite affable and the delegation left feeling that the visit had been a success. In reality, it had only symbolic significance, and there was much work to be done to protect the rights of conscience.

After significant lobbying coordinated by Paul Comly French, a birthright Friend and journalist who had been director of the Federal Writers Project and was familiar with the ways of Washington, the Selective Service and Training Act, the Burke-Wadsworth bill, did provide for persons who "by reasons of religious training and belief, are conscientiously opposed to participation in war in any form" to be placed either in noncombatant roles in the military or assigned to do work of national importance under civilian control. The provisions of the act were not as liberal as those proposed by the churches. There was no exemption for absolutists, for example, nor any provision for non-religious objectors. But the act was a significant improvement over the situation during World War I for at least two reasons. First, it broadened the definition of who could be a conscientious objector. It was no longer necessary to be a member of a recognized pacifist church, but only to have a comparable religious belief. Second, the act provided for a civilian alternative service for those whose conscience prevented them from serving in the military.

Classification decisions were delegated to the more than 6,700 local Selective Service boards around the country. A registrant who felt he qualified for CO status filed the special form for conscientious objectors, DSS Form 47, with his local board, which then made a decision. There were two types of CO classification. Those who were willing to serve in the military in a non-combatant role were classified 1-A-O; those unwilling to serve in the military were classified 4-E. An unfavorable decision could then be appealed to a Regional Board of Appeals. Under certain circumstances an adverse decision of the Regional Board of Appeals could be further appealed to the President, who delegated that authority to the Director of Selective Service. Because the decisions were made by thousands of local boards, the interpretation of the statute varied widely. Some local boards were openly hostile to COs; others, quite sympathetic.

Civilian Public Service, the network of camps and other projects where approximately twelve thousand COs performed their alternative service, was a unique and complex arrangement between the Historic Peace Churches and the Selective Service System. As described by Sibley and Jacob, "The fundamental conception of CPS was rather that of a religious order whose members, though under legal compulsion, were moved primarily by their personal ideals to perform a sacrificial service." Under an agreement worked out during the last few months of 1940, the three churches agreed to administer and finance the camps. They had proposed that the government provide the funds, but President Roosevelt's adamant opposition necessitated a compromise. To assist in this effort the Historic Peace Churches set up a cooperative organization, the National Service Board for Religious Objectors (NSBRO), chaired by M. R. Zigler of the Church of the Brethren. Additional churches and pacifist organizations, such as the Fellowship of Reconciliation and the War Resister's League, joined over years, and by the end of the war there were thirty-nine members. The Executive Secretary of the National Service Board was Paul Comly French. NSBRO was the liaison in Washington, DC, between the church groups that administered the camps and Selective Service.

The government agreed to make available abandoned Civilian Conservation Corps (CCC) camp sites and to furnish cots, bedding, and other items of camp equipment. Selective Service set policy, oversaw the operations, and paid transportation costs to the camps, just as they did for a draftee into the military. The Departments of Agriculture and Interior provided technical supervision for the work projects, as well as tools and other equipment. But the main burden fell on the three church groups: the Mennonites, Brethren, and Friends. The men received no pay for their work, nor did their dependents receive any financial assistance, unlike the dependents of those serving in the military. In fact, those who could were asked to pay $35 per month for room and board. The men received $2.50 per month in spending money. During the six years the camps operated, the churches who were members of NSBRO raised more than $7 million to support the men in CPS, along with gifts-in-kind of food, clothing, and other supplies. The bulk of this support came from the three Peace Churches even though approximately forty per cent of those in the camps claimed affiliation with other, or no, denominations. This arrangement was originally to be a six-month experiment, but it quickly became established for the duration of the war. The first CPS camp opened on May 15, 1941, in the Patapsco State Forest near Baltimore, Maryland. Although essentially all the camps were closed by the end of 1946, the CPS program officially ended on March 29, 1947.

Brethren CPS

The Brethren CPS camps were administered by the Brethren Service Committee (BSC), based in Elgin, Illinois and headed by M. R. Zigler. Initially, the national director of Brethren CPS was Dr. Paul H. Bowman, president of Bridgewater College. After a few months, Bowman was succeeded by Zigler. In February 1942 W. Harold Row, Sr. took office and continued as director for the remainder of the program. At the beginning, the office staff consisted of the director and a secretary, but eventually grew to between eighteen and twenty-five people as the demands of administering the program increased. Most of the staff were drafted COs assigned by Selective Service to the national headquarters.

The Elgin staff was responsible for all the details of the Brethren CPS program, which included representing BSC at policy meetings of the NSBRO, managing the financial aspects of the program including assistance to dependents of COs, establishing new camps, and handling the transfers of men between units. Initially the camp directors, mostly Church of the Brethren ministers, were hired by BSC. As the camps grew in size and number and the administrative needs increased, COs assigned to the camps, or "assignees," assumed most of the administrative responsibilities. Four one-month national administrative training schools were organized in 1942 and 1943. For those in Brethren camps, one week was spent in Elgin, after which they joined men from camps run by the other denominations for three weeks of sessions organized by NSBRO in Washington, D.C. By the end of the war, many camp directors were assignees chosen by the camp members themselves.

The Elgin staff also provided support to the religious and educational programs in the camps and to special projects. For many of the men, regular Sunday school classes and religious services were essential. Along with programs organized by the individual camps, the Elgin office arranged for visiting speakers who could bring an appropriate religious message to the campers. The educational programs were highly varied but usually included courses or discussions of the religious and philosophical basis of pacifism. Since attendance at the educational programs was voluntary, the courses had to respond to the needs and interests of the men to be successful, so they ranged from topics like woodworking and house building to appreciation of the fine arts. Near the end of the war, the emphasis was on demobilization: job training, placement and further education after leaving camp.[4]

For much of the war, the education director for Brethren CPS was assignee Morris T. Keeton. Originally from Texas, Keeton had recently earned the Ph.D. in philosophy at Harvard University. He was first assigned to the Brethren camp at Magnolia, Arkansas. The poet William Stafford, who bunked next to Keeton at Magnolia, remembers Keeton telling him "one of the country boys came up to him the first night, and said, 'Where are you from?' He said, 'Harvard.' He said, 'What have you been doing there?' He said, 'I've been studying for my Ph.D.,' and this country boy said, 'You ain't ever worked, have you?'"[5] Stafford

Tartt Bell (far left), unidentified CO, and Morris Keeton (far right) at the Magnolia, Arkansas, CPS camp. (*LC Stafford*)

described Keeton as the most impressive person he met in CPS "in terms of having a coherent, intellectual life and being a positive social tactics kind of person."[6] As education director Keeton worked with the individual camp education directors to develop a meaningful program. He also helped organize the special schools that were started in 1943 and 1944, including the School of Fine Arts at Waldport and the School of Pacifist Living at Cascade Locks. Keeton went on to a distinguished career in education. He served on the faculty of Antioch College from 1947 to 1977 and was the college's chief academic officer from 1963 to 1977. After leaving Antioch he served as chief executive officer of the Council on Adult and Experiential Education from 1977 to 1989, after which he became senior scholar of the Institute for Research and Assessment in Higher Education at the University of Maryland University College.[7]

When Selective Service assigned a CO to a Brethren CPS camp, the Elgin office sent him a welcoming letter that explained the philosophy of the CPS program:

> *These camps have been set up in cooperation with the United States Government to give an opportunity through cooperative good will to find a way of constructive public service. This is vital and necessary to maintain a democracy. The American way of life was developed out of ideals of equal opportunity, sacrificial good will and cooperation. While others conscientiously felt they must protect our national life and freedom with armies and offer their lives to do so; we believe we should give our best, even at sacrifice to prove democracy is the fruit of good will and self-discipline in recognizing the rights and needs of others.*

> *The essence of the Civilian Public Service program is sacrifice.
> . . . If you can visualize the significance of your work and your life in
> camp as a testimony to a way of life you will be able to prove to the
> government and to society the soundness of the philosophy of non-
> violence.*

The letter also discussed the costs:

> *The Historic Peace Churches and others are attempting to support
> these camps and estimate the cost at $35.00 per month per man. You
> can help much in economy and care of the property. All who believe in
> this philosophy of life and helpfulness can do much by some sacrifice of
> themselves, of their families, friends and churches to help support the
> work financially, that it may reach its highest significance to ourselves
> and others.*[8]

The final paragraph gave the name and mailing address of the
director of the camp to which the man had been assigned, in case the
assignee wanted to contact him before arriving.[9] Men were usually
assigned to camps close to their place of induction, but at least one
hundred miles away. Since the place of induction was usually near
the man's home, the hundred-mile rule was adopted to make sure
they could not return home on weekends. The men also received a
list of things to bring, particularly work clothes and gloves. Because
they were to live in dormitories with limited storage space they were
encouraged not to bring much.

Along with a letter of welcome, a CO received a voucher for
transportation to the camp from Selective Service. He said goodbye to
family and friends, boarded a train or bus to a station near the camp,
and began a new life. In 1941 when the first men arrived at camps
throughout the United States, they expected to spend a year doing
"work of national importance." After Pearl Harbor, the United States
entered the war and their term became the duration of the war plus six
months, the same as for those who entered the military.

CHAPTER THREE

The First Months: Organizing a Community

Civilian Public Service Camp #21 at Cascade Locks, Oregon, officially opened on November 27, 1941, when nine men arrived, transfers from the CPS camp at San Dimas, California. They were welcomed by the camp director, the Reverend Mark Y. Schrock, and two COs who were already there, J. Henry Dasenbrock and Wayne Gregory. Dasenbrock had known Mark Schrock while growing up in Fruitland, Idaho, where Schrock was serving as the minister of the Brethren Church in nearby Nampa. When Dasenbrock learned that Schrock was the director of the CPS camp to which he had been assigned, he volunteered to help with the preparations. Schrock was living in Olympia, Washington, where he had been minister of the Church of the Brethren congregation prior to volunteering to work with Brethren CPS; Dasenbrock came to Olympia and slept on the living room couch for several weeks before traveling to Cascade Locks to help ready the camp.[1] Since Wayne Gregory was a member of Schrock's congregation in Olympia, he had also been available for work in the early weeks.

The site at Cascade Locks had been a Civilian Conservation Corps (CCC) camp which Mark Schrock had chosen because it had excellent facilities, was easy to reach by road or rail, and had a wide variety of Forest Service work projects in the Mount Hood National Forest. It was a spectacular site, located on Gorton Creek with the Columbia River to the north and the walls of the Columbia River gorge to the south. By the time the camp opened Schrock had spent a year preparing for this assignment. In early winter 1940 he and his family traveled to Brethren, Michigan, for several months of CPS training. After they returned to Olympia, Schrock in-

(*LC Schrock 3*)

J. Henry Dasenbrock posting a notice on the camp bulletin board. (*Davis-Kovac*)

View of CPS #21 from the south. The dining hall is in the foreground and dormitories to the right. The Columbia River and Wind Mountain are in the background. (*LC Schrock 1*)

vestigated several possible camp sites in the Northwest before settling on Cascade Locks.[2]

The evening of December 5, seventy-one men arrived by train from California. Dasenbrock and others from the camp met them in the dark at the Cascade Locks railroad station and brought them to the camp in Forest Service trucks. The camp was actually located at Wyeth,

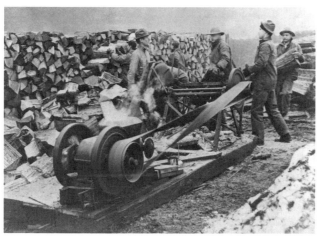

Firewood splitting crew. (*Davis-Kovac*)

about eight miles east of Cascade Locks. Over the next seven weeks the camp population grew to 105. Eventually, the camp housed about two hundred men, and approximately 560 spent some time there before it closed in July 1946, making it the largest camp in the CPS system. (A complete roster can be found in the Appendix.) It was also in service longer than any other camp in the Brethren system.

Much of the first seven weeks was consumed with cutting and splitting wood to feed the endless appetite of the more than thirty-five wood stoves that provided the only warmth for the camp. As Mark Schrock wrote, "Through fog, rain, wind, and snow the relentless crews swarm and toil like pack rats driven by a collecting habit that has become obsession."[3] Schrock estimated that nearly five hundred cords of wood were cut and ricked.

In mid-December 1941 a side camp was established on nearby Larch Mountain. About twenty volunteers from the main camp at Wyeth, led by assistant director Albert Bohrer, moved to a small, rundown CCC camp partway up the road from the Columbia River Highway to the summit of Larch Mountain. The main reasons for the side camp were to put crews closer to areas of potential forest fires, and to build and staff a new fire lookout tower on the top of Larch Mountain. Later, a smaller lookout tower was also constructed on nearby Pepper Mountain. Early work at the side camp included renovating the camp and cutting firewood for the winter, but felling snags (dead trees that were considered serious fire hazards) and planting trees soon became

Larch Mountain Side Camp. (*Davis-Kovac*)

Building the fire lookout tower on Larch Mountain. (*Davis-Kovac*)

the major activities along with building the lookout towers. These activities were directed by an enthusiastic forest service supervisor, Brit Ash. Eventually the Larch Mountain side camp housed as many as forty-five men.

Keeping warm and dry was a major problem. As Charlie Davis wrote, "Wyeth gets more rainfall annually than Portland or Hood River. In fact, except for coastal areas it is the wettest place in the state. When the winter winds are blowing from Idaho down the Gorge, it is also the coldest with the most ice."[4] As Davis, who had just graduated from the University of Southern California noted, many of the men from California found the first winter very depressing.

The Wyeth camp consisted of four dormitories, each with space for fifty to sixty men. Other buildings included a dining hall and kitchen; an administration building; two cottages, one for the director and another for the Forest Service ranger; an infirmary, laundry and latrines; a recreation hall; and several buildings related to the work projects. Under the direction of COs Kemper Nomland, an architect and artist who had recently graduated from the University of Southern California, and Alan McRae, an architect from Seattle, the men had turned one of the buildings on the site into an attractive library with a reading room, a periodical room, a music room, two classrooms for the educational program, and offices for the librarian and the newspaper. The library featured indirect lighting and was eventually decorated with artwork by the campers, including Kemper Nomland's portrait of Mark Schrock, which was hung in the reading room. The music room was equipped with a good record player where the records brought to camp could be played.[5] They also renovated the old CCC chapel by installing a floor-to-ceiling window at the end of the building that faced the mountains, and dividing the window into four parts with a gold cross. The chapel became one of the highlights of the camp and served as the site for weddings of CPS men over the years. J. Henry Dasenbrock, who had worked as a professional photographer, constructed a small darkroom in one corner of the wood shop and encouraged members of the camp to become interested in photography. The photos taken by Dasenbrock and Henry Blocher provide important documentation of the life at CPS #21.[6]

The accommodations were quite spartan, but the men did what they could to make them more comfortable. The dorms were painted with bright colors. Beds were arranged in informal groupings; some were made into double-deckers to provide additional living space, which was furnished with home-made chairs. The dorms quickly obtained names: Duration Hall, the Wigwam, Sleepy Hollow, and Bar-barracks.[7] The creative arrangement of the dorms was a continual source of irritation to the Selective Service inspectors who were officers in the military and thought the dorms should look like military barracks. Another factor that added to the positive atmosphere of the camp was the presence of the Schrock family. Mabel Schrock and the four children, Jeanne

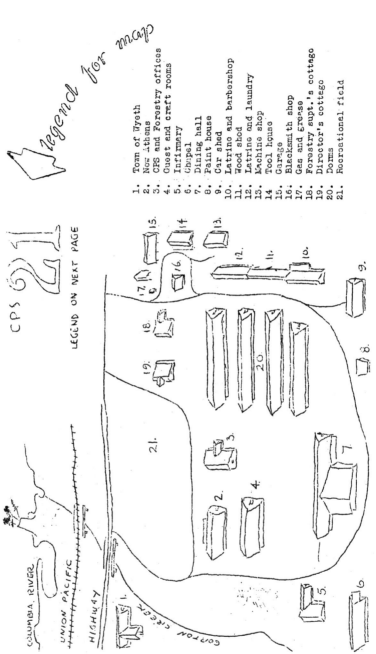

Legend for map

1. Town of Wyeth
2. New Athens
3. CPS and Forestry offices
4. Guest and craft rooms
5. Infirmary
6. Chapel
7. Dining hall
8. Paint house
9. Car shed
10. Latrine and barbershop
11. Wood shed
12. Latrine and laundry
13. Machine shop
14. Tool house
15. Garage
16. Blacksmith shop
17. Gas and grease
18. Forestry supt.'s cottage
19. Director's cottage
20. Dorms
21. Recreational field

CPS 21

LEGEND ON NEXT PAGE

COLUMBIA RIVER

UNION PACIFIC

HIGHWAY

GORTON CREEK

Camp map showing the location along Gorton Creek and the layout of
the buildings. (*Davis-Kovac*)

(age ten), Julian (nine), Grace (seven), and Gladden (five), arrived from Olympia on December 21, 1941, and moved into the small director's cottage. The cottage, however, did not have a kitchen, so the Schrocks ate all their meals in the camp dining hall, which meant they were a constant presence. As Julian Schrock remembers, several campers paid a lot of attention to the Schrock children. For example, Paul Kindy, a Brethren from Middlebury, Indiana, who was distantly related to Mark Schrock, spent most of his time at Cascade Locks on kitchen duty, so he had free time between meals. In the summers he often rounded up the kids and took them swimming in the Columbia River. Gilbert Grover, an Old German Baptist from Modesto, California, read to the children in his off-duty hours. Hugh Merrick, a talented violinist who had played with the San Francisco Symphony, sometimes played duets with Mabel Schrock, who was a fine pianist. Jeanne Schrock took violin lessons from Merrick.[8] Richard Anderson remembers "the children's presence in the camp added a wonderful feeling of home life in the middle of the Oregon woods. They helped us feel that we were still at 'home.'"[9]

When it opened, the camp had only two paid staff members: Mark Schrock, the director, and a dietitian, Mary Eiler. Albert Bohrer, an assignee with school teaching experience, served as assistant director, and Frank Neufeld, another assignee, served as business manager. Originally, CPS #21 was jointly administered by the Brethren Service Committee and the Mennonite Central Committee. The churches had thought the camps they administered would primarily serve their own members, an expectation that was quickly proven to be false as men from dozens of other denominations received the 4-E classification and were assigned to the various camps. Since CPS #21 was the only camp in the Northwest, the joint administration seemed sensible and Bohrer, a Mennonite, was sent to the camp to be assistant director and represent Mennonite Central Committee. The joint sponsorship soon proved to be administratively inconvenient and CPS #21 became strictly a Brethren camp in May 1942. Mary Eiler departed after just a few weeks, largely because there was no suitable place for her to live at the camp, and Mabel Schrock filled the role of dietician working with the kitchen staff. For the next six months the two Schrocks were the only paid employees. In June 1942, Maude Gregory from Olympia, whose son was in the camp, was employed as "camp matron" and eventually as dietitian replacing Mabel Schrock.

Rev. Mark Y. Schrock with the portrait painted by Kemper Nomland. (*LC Blocher D19*)

Columbia Chapel, designed by Kemper Nomland. (*LC Schrock 18*)

The tasks of running the camp were performed by the assignees themselves as camp "overhead." Three men worked in the office: one as business manager, one as clerk for official matters, and a third handling informal relationships. At the beginning, there was a kitchen and dining hall staff of ten: five cooks and bakers, and five who waited tables, washed dishes and kept records. These latter were known as KPs, using the military terminology. Two men operated the laundry, doing all the washing and ironing. New arrivals were given a long string of numbers to sew onto every article of clothing that they owned, even the socks, so they could be identified and sorted by the laundry crew. One man had charge of the infirmary, administering first aid, caring for the sick and assisting the camp doctor. Mark Schrock had arranged for a retired pediatrician, Dr. Stone, who lived near the camp, to take care of the camp's medical needs. Some people in the community suggested that Dr. Stone had become a veterinarian because he was

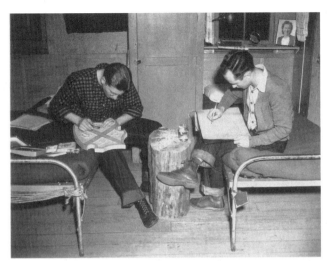

Unidentified COs in the dorm at CPS #21. (*Davis-Kovac*)

The Schrock Family, Mark, Mabel, Julian, Gladden, Grace and Jeanne, in the Director's Cottage at Cascade Locks. (*Davis-Kovac*)

"taking care of all those horses' asses in the camp."[10] One assignee was the equipment manager, and four others were responsible for camp maintenance, including splitting and hauling wood for the voracious stoves. As the camp grew the number of overhead positions permitted by Selective Service regulations increased. By early summer 1942 the population was nearly two hundred, and the laundry crew had expanded to four. As men entered camp or were transferred to other CPS camps or sent to side camps, the individuals holding the various jobs changed as well.

Camp office at Cascade Locks with COs (from left) Bob Case, Mel Holt, Al Bohrer, Jim Martin and Al Hastings. (*LC Blocher D28*)

Laundry crew: (from left) Kermit Sheets, Wirt Fairman and Dub Lowber. (*Brethren*)

Another dozen men were assigned to Forest Service overhead, where the jobs included sharpening tools and blacksmith work. Julian Schrock remembers spending time watching the saw sharpener, Danny Stutzman, filing and setting the teeth on the large two-man saws. The same man also cared for and sharpened the other tools such as axes and pulaskis. For a time the blacksmith at Cascade Locks was Rene Arroyo, a Catholic from San Francisco. Arroyo was married and his wife had come to Oregon with him, so he spent as much time with her as possible and was not very involved in camp activities. He spent his days at the forge repairing log chains, tools, truck parts and farm equipment.[11]

Charlie Davis worked in the Forest Service office. In a letter to family and friends in July 1942 he described his work:

Regarding my particular occupation. I have the choice job of the lot — pretty lucky. I function as clerk to the District Ranger, which is mighty interesting work. Typing is one of the duties, operating a radio, a telephone switchboard, recording the weather, platting fires, map making, janitor work, filing (clerical and mechanical), fire building and flag raising, are all in my line of activity. Starting July 1, with the beginning of dry weather, I have been dashing around like a mad man. There are 32 Forest Service employees in addition to the 201 CPS men working on this district and their problems seem all to come over my desk on route to the ranger. I have never seen anyone that is expected to be more diversified than a ranger. He has to have a smattering of just about everything from Governmental Accounting to Forest Fire Fighting, so I have learned a little in the seven months here. The ranger is a wonderful person, and I have enjoyed working for him, even if it is at my own expense.[12]

The rest of the men in camp were engaged in work assigned by the Forest Service ranger, such as road and trail construction, camp ground maintenance, telephone line work, snag felling, and fire fighting.[13] Each morning there was a work call at 7:20 A.M., and the men gathered at the Forest Service office to learn their assignments for the day. Ordinarily they were transported to the work sites in Forest Service vehicles and returned at the end of the workday for dinner. A foot-locker containing lunches was loaded onto the truck. Lunch usually consisted of three

Charlie Davis working in the Forest Service Office. (*Davis-Kovac*)

Early morning work call at Cascade Locks. The COs were
transported by truck to the work site every morning. (*LC Blocher
D62*)

sandwiches: one with peanut butter, a second with jam, and third with
lunch meat or cheese. Don Smith remembers that during his time at
camp one of the sandwiches always seemed to be filled with home-
made prune jam, probably donated, which he described as "burnt
prune jam." During the rainy winter someone would start a fire and
the men would gather around it to warm up and eat their sandwiches.
Some would find sharp sticks and toast their sandwiches over the fire,
resulting in a burnt bottom and a soggy top. At the end of the day, the
dinners in the Wyeth dining hall were plentiful and tasty.[14]

The daily routine of three sandwiches for lunch soon became boring.
One day, when the men loaded the footlocker onto the truck they
noticed a sign that read *Hebrews* 13:8. No one on that crew remembered
the verse but when they returned that evening they raced for their
Bibles and found the quotation, "Jesus Christ, the same yesterday,
today, and forever."[15]

Some assignments, however, kept men in the field for several days
at a time. For example, in June 1942 Henry Dasenbrock and Leland
Goodell spent five days walking fifty-five miles of trails pushing a
bicycle wheel to measure distances. They also compiled a report on
the conditions of the trails and Forest Service buildings. The camp
newspaper the *Columbian* for January 30, 1942 lists some of the work

projects under way. A six-man crew was clearing logs from the nearby Bonneville Power right of way and bringing the wood to camp where it was sawed and ricked. Another crew was involved in maintenance of Eagle Creek park. Finally, four men were rebuilding a stone wall at the ranger station.[16]

The same pattern of work continued for the remainder of the war. About a third of the work was connected with preventing or fighting fires, including building and maintaining roads and trails, building fire breaks, reducing fire hazards by removing snags and brush, building and maintaining lookout towers, and the organizing, training, and managing and equipping of fire suppression units. Another third of the work involved constructing buildings, bridges, fences, and even a dam. Considerable effort was expended in constructing and repairing telephone lines. There was a sign shop at Cascade Locks where COs made and painted signs for the forests around the Northwest. Trees were planted in areas devastated by forest fires, and new public campgrounds were developed. The men also worked in forest service nurseries. Some were trained as timber estimators and made surveys of available lumber. From time to time the men were called out for emergency farm work, particularly harvesting fruit in the nearby Hood River valley.[17]

Wilmer Carlson and Kemper Nomland building the rock wall behind the ranger station near the camp. (*Brethren*)

Camp Government and Activities

One of Mark Schrock's early goals was to develop a democratic government to organize the life of the camp within the constraints of the Selective Service regulations. Although the work hours, time off and leave privileges were tightly controlled, other aspects of camp life were left to the discretion of the director and Mark Shrock's leadership style was facilitative rather than dictatorial. Almost immediately a camp council was elected with J. Henry Dasenbrock as president. The first camp council also included Eugene Hudson, Walter Haag, Hugh Merrick, Charlie Davis, Al Benglen, Bill Cable, and Gladden Boaz. One of the major tasks of the camp council was to develop a more permanent governmental structure, and a constitution committee was established. The president appointed committees on religion, education, and recreation. A sanitation committee under the direction of Mabel Schrock was established to "direct and assist" men in keeping the camp neat.

Within a month the COs, in cooperation with the director, began to hold regular religious services. On Sundays several classes were offered including a discussion of the bases for pacifism and a Bible study group giving particular attention to the literary qualities. These classes were followed by a non-denominational worship service. There was also a Wednesday evening prayer meeting. The Jehovah's Witnesses in the camp held a regular Bible study of their own.

The education program developed a bit more slowly, but by mid-February an extensive selection of evening classes had been organized. Three fifty-minute class periods were designated: 7:00, 7:50, and 8:40 P.M., Monday through Friday. Men who were interested in a particular course were invited to meet, suggest a plan of study, a teacher, and a time to the educational committee, which was chaired by Kermit Sheets. If the committee approved, the class was fitted into the camp schedule. The first courses included first aid, fireguard training, chorus, safety, photography, woodworking, and art appreciation. Director Mark Schrock, a graduate of Manchester College, offered a class in the Bible. As profiles of the faculty show, the camp included men of remarkable talent. For example, Bill Henderson, who taught an appreciation of fine arts class, was an accomplished cellist who had been a music, philosophy and literature major for three years at Pomona College before being drafted. Violinist Hugh Merrick offered a class in music reading.

First camp council meeting in the dining hall: (from left) Eugene Hudson, Walter Haag, Hugh Merrick, Charles Davis, Al Benglen, Bill Cable, Gladden Boaz and J. Henry Dasenbrock. (*Davis-Kovac*)

Mark Schrock teaching Bible. (*LC Blocher D20*)

Don Baker and
Kemper Nomland
printing *The
Columbian.* (*LC
Blocher D31*)

Hugh Merrick. (*Brethren*)

Many CPS camps published newspapers; the one at Cascade Locks was called *The Columbian*. Its first issue appeared on January 30, 1942. The editorial staff, led by Wendell Harmon who had worked for the *Los Angeles Times* prior to being drafted, promised bi-weekly publication and offered one-year subscriptions to "friends of CPS" — twenty-six issues for 75¢.[18] Publication of the first issue was a big event. Kermit Sheets, who was the assistant editor, enlisted Julian and Gladden Schrock as newspaper boys. Decked out with signs pinned to their shirts and with crazy hats, they came into the dining hall to distribute papers. Julian rode the Schrock family bicycle down the aisles with a paper-carrier's canvas bag over his shoulder. Gladden had to walk, but he also had a bag of papers. Julian remembers having trouble steering because of the weight of the bag on his left shoulder. The paper was mimeographed, double-sided, on 11" by 17" sheets and folded to produce an 8½" by 11" final product.[19] Eventually, eighteen issues of the *Columbian* would appear before it ceased publication in February of 1943.

The *Columbian* shows that the men of CPS #21 had a vibrant cultural and recreational life. Vocalist Allen Hastings, a graduate of the University of Southern California School of Music, organized a chorus that rehearsed twice a week. There were regular concerts featuring camp musicians. Among the arrivals during the first year were pianist Harry Prochaska, violinist Hugh Merrick, cellist Bill Henderson, flautist Windsor Utley, and vibraphonist and pianist Bob Searles. Leland Goodell was a classically trained baritone who had been a finalist in auditions for the Metropolitan Opera. Bill Phillips was also a fine singer. In addition there was a sports program: ping pong, horseshoes, softball, and basketball. The first issue of the *Columbian* reports that CPS basketball team lost to Cascade Locks High School 26-24 in a game played in the high school gym on January 17. Editor Wendell Harmon was the high scorer with 10 points. For the less active, the recreation hall had two sets of checkers. There appears to have been little card playing, although a small group got together regularly to play bridge. Several men including Kermit Sheets and Don Baker, who were regular readers of the *New Yorker,* pooled their money to pay for a subscription. When the issues came, they took turns reading the articles aloud to each other.[20]

The constitution committee did its work efficiently and on February 16, 1942, the camp unanimously adopted a permanent plan of government which called for a camp council consisting of a president, vice-president, secretary, and six committee chairmen. All members of the council were to be elected at-large except the vice-president, who was to be elected by the council. The first officers were Bill Phillips, president, and Wendell Taylor, secretary, with six committee chairmen: George Maurer, recreation; Kermit Sheets, education; Jacob Quiring, religious; Bernard Good, housekeeping; Wendell Harmon, editorial board; and Art Franz, safety. The council also included one representative from each of the four dorms. The method of election was complicated. There were to be no nominations; each man was to vote for the person he thought most qualified for the position by secret ballot. If no one received a majority, then a second balloting was held among the top candidates, as many as needed to have the sum of their votes be a majority. This process was repeated until someone received a majority. The officers served terms of four months.

Despite the unanimous vote, protests against the new government arose almost immediately. There were several reasons for this tension. First, the government was not working very well. Democracy is inefficient and meetings could become extremely long. Participation lagged; men who had spent the day in hard physical labor were often too tired to do much in the evening. Second, some of the more conservative members of the camp, particularly the Mennonites, were not interested in democratic government. They would have preferred for the director and staff to make decisions. On the other hand, there were others who felt that the government should have more authority, and that the director and other staff members should be democratically elected or, at least, that the camp should have an elected representative on the staff. Perhaps most important was that COs are an independent-minded group. As time went on the reality of conscription became clear. That they were compelled to engage in what began to seem like meaningless work became the essential reality of their lives, and conflict with authority, in the form of the director, the Brethren Service Committee, the Forest Service, and the Selective Service, was more frequent as they tried to make the administration of the camp more compatible with their philosophy. Eventually, these tensions resulted in a significant change in the administration and government of the camp.[21]

Like Wyeth, the Larch Mountain camp almost immediately established a temporary camp government structure with a camp president, camp council, and committees on religious life, education, and recreation. The terms of office were set at three months and the committees began to develop an educational program with courses in safety, first aid, woodcarving, photography, and Bible study. A chorus was formed under the direction of Harry Prochaska. During the first months, the men at Larch Mountain returned to Wyeth on weekends to participate in the social and religious activities, but as the side camp's population grew, it became increasingly independent and self-contained. In the June 6, 1942, issue of the *Columbian*, Harry Prochaska called them "a peculiar people," a small, isolated, close-knit group which he contrasted with the more worldly, sophisticated society in the main camp at Wyeth. Perhaps they were unsophisticated, but they did have a vocal recital by bass-baritone Leland Goodell, accompanied by

Harry Prochaska on piano, on May 23, and staged a farewell banquet with entertainment for Brit Ash and his wife on June 13. Early issues of the *Columbian* included news from Larch Mountain, but by June the men at Larch were publishing their own newspaper, eventually named *The Larch Mountaineer.*

As the main camp grew, Al Bohrer was called back to help with administration, and a new assistant director was appointed from among the side camp membership. Initially, George Maurer served as first aid man and assistant director. After Maurer returned to Wyeth, Dwight Hanawalt replaced him. Hanawalt was a graduate of La Verne College, a Church of the Brethren institution in Southern California. After the war he returned to La Verne to help revitalize the athletic program. He spent forty years at La Verne as professor of physical education, intercollegiate coach, chair of the Department of Health, Physical Education and Recreation, and as dean of students. When he retired from what had become the University of La Verne in 1986, his distinguished service was recognized with an honorary doctorate. After Hanawalt transferred to the CPS project in Puerto Rico, Douglas C. Strain became the side camp leader.[22]

When the United States entered World War II in December 1941, Doug Strain was a junior at Cal Tech, a transfer from Pasadena Junior College. Because he had received the 4-E classification as a CO, he was summoned to the registrar's office where he was informed that all Cal Tech students were required to join ROTC. When he refused he was informed that he would not be allowed to stay in school and finish the term. Strain appealed to Linus Pauling, the Cal Tech chemist who would eventually win two Nobel Prizes, one for chemistry and the other for peace. Pauling intervened with the administration and Strain was allowed to take his exams and finish the term, but early in 1942 he was on his way to Cascade Locks. In 1943 he transferred to the camp at Walhalla, Michigan, to participate in the School of Cooperative Living, a systematic study group organized by Brethren CPS under the supervision of Morris Mitchell, then participated in a medical experiment at the University of Illinois. For the last year of his CPS service he was assigned to the Forest Service Experimental Radio Lab in Portland. After the war Strain returned to Cal Tech to complete his degree in electrical engineering and eventually to Portland where he founded ElectroScientific Industries, a small company that developed and manufactured electronic test equipment.[23]

Although room and board were provided, the men needed to obtain personal items such as toiletries, stationery and work gloves at a reasonable cost. To fill these needs a cooperative store was established, consistent with the ideals of many of the COs. As articulated in an article in *The Columbian* for March 28, 1942, the store operated on the seven Rochdale principles.[24] These principles derived from those set down from the Rochdale Society of Equitable Pioneers established in England in 1844. The members of this society came from a broad spectrum of political and religious beliefs and their principles became the foundation of future cooperative movements.[25]

1. *Open membership. No camp member will be excluded from participating.*
2. *Democratic control. A board of directors will be chosen by the campers to operate the store.*
3. *Dividend on purchases. Each participant's earnings will be determined by the amount purchased.*
4. *Limited interest on capital. The periodic returns to participants will be determined by the economic equilibrium of the store.*
5. *Political and religious neutrality. All creeds may enjoy equal participation.*
6. *Cash payment. No purchase shall be made and charged.*
7. *Promotion of education.*

A secure space for the store was created in the recreation building. The article reported that it was doing very well, and it continued until the camp closed in 1946.

To reduce food costs and provide fresh produce, milk, eggs and meat, the camp rented a nearby farm in March 1942. The thirty-acre farm about a quarter-mile west of the camp had around twenty-five acres of tillable land and five acres suitable for grazing. It also had an orchard with both apple and cherry trees. One of the campers, Elzie Holderreed, became the first full-time farm manager, but other campers were assigned to help at busy times of the year.[26] A second, much larger farm to the west was rented later that year. Because of the difference in elevation, the first farm was known as the lower farm and the second as the upper. The two farms produced vegetables and fruit for the camp, some of which were canned for later use. The camp also purchased fruit from local orchards for canning. Hogs, dairy and beef cattle, rabbits, and chickens were raised to provide meat, milk, and eggs. Eventually, the dairy supplied the camp with an ample amount

Raymond Verbeck working on the camp farm. (*Brethren*)

of milk; the camp was even criticized by Colonel Franklin L. McLean of the camp operations division of Selective Service for using too much milk. The farms also provided a place for campers who came from an agricultural background to work. Because of the farms, the food at Cascade Locks was both good and plentiful.[27]

By April of 1942 CPS #21 had become a fully functioning camp. The new camp government had been established, and educational, religious and recreational programs were under way. The library, which contained about fifteen hundred volumes and subscribed to thirty-four periodicals, had been named the Mark Schrock Library in honor of the director. The beautifully renovated Columbia Chapel had been dedicated on Easter Sunday. A farm had been rented to provide food for the camp. The men were prepared for one of their major tasks of the summer: fighting forest fires. They had a small taste of what was to come when they were called to help fight a 160-acre fern fire on Larch Mountain on March 30.[28] But the same issue of the *Columbian* that told the story of the first fire also contained a list of new arrivals to the camp. One of them would make Cascade Locks the best-known CPS camp in the country.

Lew Ayres

On March 30, 1942, the film actor Lew Ayres boarded a train for Wyeth to report to CPS #21. A private man, Ayres avoided curious spectators by catching the train at San Fernando, a flag stop in the Los Angeles suburbs. Although not a member of a church, he had been classified as a conscientious objector (4-E) by Selective Service Board 246, in response to a long and detailed statement of his beliefs. His deeply spiritual nature and passionate commitment to non-violence are evident in statements such as "I also believe it to be sinful, and in opposition to Man's mission on Earth, to assist others in killing or in using violence. And thus I am constrained, by my conscience, to refuse to participate in any non-combatant work that has the destruction of human life as its final consequences." Ayres understood that his position would be unpopular but he stood firm: "And were I now, through fear of public opinion or avarice, to stifle even momentarily the compulsion of my inner beliefs, the net result would be no less a lie to others than a lie to myself. A superb hypocrisy embracing for me, the shallow, animal existence of a life without honor—a life without ideals."[29] As he left Los Angeles, Ayres knew that he might be leaving his movie career behind.

Lew Ayres's biggest role had been as the disillusioned young German soldier Paul Baumer in Milestone's 1930 pacifist classic, *All Quiet on the Western Front*. Between 1931 and the United States entry into World

Lew Ayers, Dr. Stone and William McReynolds in the infirmary. (*LC Blocher D39*)

War II in December 1941, he appeared in forty-six films, including the popular Young Doctor Kildare series where he played opposite Lionel Barrymore. His decision to seek CO status and his assignment to Cascade Locks received national attention. A United Press wire story on his departure was published in the *New York Times* on March 31 and also in the Portland *Oregonian,* so his arrival at Cascade Locks was widely known in the local community.[30] Julian Schrock remembers his schoolteacher asking him, "This is a big day at your camp, isn't it?" and then jokingly asking if she could go home with him after school.[31] Had she gone to the camp she probably would have been disappointed. Ayres's arrival didn't create a stir; he was introduced just like any other new assignee.

Ayres's CO stance was controversial; editorial writers and columnists attacked him. Many called him unpatriotic; others condemned him for not measuring up to the ideals of manhood.[32] His films were picketed and banned. An editorial in the *Washington Post* on April 5, however, praised him as an example of "great moral courage" and pointed out that his career as an actor was likely to suffer. As a Hollywood star he could have chosen to join the military where his talents would probably have gained him a relatively easy life, making films or entertaining troops. Instead he chose to go into CPS to do manual labor. The *Post* concluded the editorial by saying that they disagreed with Ayres's position but wondered whether those who supported the war were "willing to make as many sacrifices for their convictions as Ayres and the other conscientious objectors have made for theirs."[33]

At Cascade Locks Ayres primarily worked in the infirmary and taught first aid. In his statement to his draft board, he had requested that he be drafted into the medical or hospital corps or the Red Cross service, and noted that he was fitted for both services "in a small way." Ayres had attended the University of Arizona, planning to become a physician, but had dropped out to pursue a career in music. He was a talented banjo and guitar player and a pianist. An agent discovered Ayres playing in a Hollywood nightclub, which led to his movie career. Still interested in health care, he had been a volunteer Red Cross first aid instructor for some time before the war. His portrayal of Dr. Kildare in the film series was also influential in his determination to work as a medic.[34]

During his time at Cascade Locks, Ayres began to make inquiries about transferring to non-combatant service, but only in the medical corps. According to an article in the May 23, 1942, issue of the *Columbian,* Ayres was unaware of the 1-A-O classification when he originally applied for his CO status, which was why he received the 4-E classification. Julian Schrock remembers another story, that Ayres's Hollywood draft board wanted to embarrass him and did not allow him to register as a non-combatant in the medical corps, although his CO statement clearly states that such service was his preference. An article in *The Washington Post* of April 10, 1942, provides support for this second version with the comment, "Ayres said last week on entering the Cascade Locks 'C.O.' camp that he had been refused permission to enter the corps."

Ayres's petitions eventually resulted in a "'verbal assurance' from Selective Service that he would be assigned medical noncombatant duties exclusively."[35] On April 10, 1942, a front-page story in the *Washington Post* led with the statement, "Selective Service Director Lewis B. Hershey said last night that Lew Ayres, Hollywood movie star now in a conscientious objectors' camp at Cascade Locks, Oreg, probably will be reclassified for non-combatant duty if he can pass Army physical requirements." By May 18, Ayres's petition had been granted, and the *New York Times* contained an article indicating that Ayres would be assigned to an Army Medical Corps unit the following day. "'There is one thing I want understood,' Ayres said in a statement, 'And that is there has been no change in my thoughts or theories. I am grateful for reassignment, however, for the Medical Corps is the place I want to be — to be able to do some useful work.'"[36]

In his short time at Cascade Locks, Lew Ayres did not ask for or receive special privileges. He carried out his work assignment enthusiastically. A strict vegetarian, he "inspired a table for non-carnivores which threatened to overflow."[37] He mainly kept to himself, reading and answering stacks of mail, but got along well with the other men. Before Ayres's arrival the camp received one bag of mail per day; during his time the daily delivery was three bags. The *Columbian* characterizes him as "always friendly, often dogmatic, [and] sometimes stagy." Charlie Davis remembers that Lew Ayres was the first person he had known who wore a scarf to keep his neck warm. When other men in camp adopted this style, they were accused of "putting on Ayres."

He built a strong relationship with Mark Schrock. Ayres was a serious student of religion, and the two of them had many discussions on religious belief and practice. As a result they became quite close friends. Schrock, however, disagreed with Ayres's decision to join the Army Medical Corps.[38] On August 18, 1942, Schrock received a handwritten letter from Ayres who was then at Camp Barkeley in Texas. In this letter he indicated that he had been treated well by the Army since leaving Cascade Locks, but that he did miss the men at the camp, "even my most worthy opponents — the Socialists." Ayres went on to reaffirm his stand, "I am a *CO*!! Staunch! Confirmed!" and to say to Schrock, "I hope we will one day cooperate on a constructive project of mutual interest, though until we know the outcome of this present war it is hard to predict what type of project will be most effective."[39] A newspaper clipping from the *Fort Worth Star-Telegram*, dated August 16, 1942, with the headline, "Conscientious Objector Ayres is Making Uncle Sam a Good Soldier," accompanied the letter. A similar article also appeared in the *New York Times* the same day. Mark Schrock answered at length but not until April 22, 1943. Schrock's letter includes a lot of news about members of the camp, but also includes Schrock's reflections on his difficult role as director and his increasing desire to leave CPS and return to a farm in Indiana where he could lead a more normal family life.[40]

Lew Ayres served in the Pacific theater with distinction as medical corps technician in a mobile evacuation unit and as a chaplain's assistant. He showed courage under fire in three beachhead landings with invasion forces and received three battle stars. In these invasions he was the only medic to go into battle unarmed, and when the wounded were brought in he was as attentive to the Japanese as to the Americans. As Paul Fussell says, he was much admired: "Oh, the soldiers admired Lew Ayres, actually, because he was the most publicized CO in the country. . . . And the troops I dealt with thought he was terrific. They envied him. They wished they had thought of it."[41]

After the war he returned to Hollywood to rehabilitate his career, receiving an Academy Award nomination for his role in *Johnny Belinda* in 1948. In 1955 he produced a documentary film, *Altars of the East*, recounting a trip through Asia to study the non-Christian religions of the Far East. A book with the same title was published in 1956.[42] He produced a second documentary on world religions, *Altars of the World*, in 1976. Ayres continued to appear in films and on television until his retirement in 1985. He died in Los Angeles in December 1996.

As the article in the *Columbian* points out, "[T]he most significant factor is not the impression Ayres left at Camp 21; it is the publicity he has given the entire CPS movement. The isolationist CO finds the notoriety bad; the evangelistic CO finds it good. The point is, however, now that the civilian public servant is familiar to the public, he must act constructively, and act now."[43] Lew Ayres certainly brought the CO cause to the public's attention, but equally importantly, he opened up opportunities for COs who wanted to serve as medics in the military. Before Ayres, the 1A-O had to accept whatever non-combatant service the military decided he should have. After Ayres, it was possible to make a request and have it honored.[44]

During Lew Ayres's time at Cascade Locks, the camp received a visit from Colonel Lewis F. Kosch, the Director of Camp Operations for Selective Service, who inspected the work project and spoke to a large gathering of campers. Kosch brought two major messages. First, Selective Service was in complete control of their lives. "The assignees are in reality available to the government 24 hours a day; and in case of emergency, the men may be called upon to work whenever the Project Superintendent requires them. Any time off that is granted to the campers should be considered a privilege, not a right." Second, "We must keep out of the limelight and avoid public contacts if we are to eliminate an antagonistic public opinion." Kosch concluded by threatening, "The government can at any time take over the operation of the CPS camps; but it is satisfied with their present operation, and as long as the churches can continue to run them satisfactorily, the government will not accept the obligation."[45] Neither Colonel Kosch nor the men of CPS #21 realized that events would soon embroil the camp in a controversy that would threaten to bring down the entire Civilian Public Service system.

CHAPTER FOUR

Summer and Fall 1942: Confrontations

As summer approached, CPS #21 saw many changes. Men continued to arrive, increasing the size of the camp, but others left, including two assignees who were staff members, and some camp leaders. For example, in late April, twenty-six men, mainly Mennonites, including Wendell Harmon, editor of *The Columbian*, and business manager Frank Neufeld, were transferred to the new Mennonite Camp in Placerville, California. The same week, twenty-nine new men arrived. On May 22, 1942, the Mennonite Central Committee withdrew from joint administration of the camp, leaving it entirely in the hands of the Brethren Service Committee. The two churches had originally set up several joint camps, but this arrangement proved to be administratively inconvenient, so an agreement was worked out in which the BSC administered CPS #21 and the MCC took sole control of the camp at Marietta, OH. Mennonites at Cascade Locks were given the opportunity to transfer to Mennonite camps if they preferred. Many took that opportunity, and the overall composition of the camp became increasingly religiously diverse. Within a few months, Assistant Director Albert Bohrer would also leave Cascade Locks, completing the transition to Brethren control. Recognizing that Brethren and Mennonites had become a minority in the camp, Mark Schrock was careful to choose new staff members from other religious backgrounds.

After the war, Wendell Harmon edited a volume of memoirs by men from the Brethren in Christ who served in CPS entitled *They Also Serve*.[1] He earned a Ph.D. in history at UCLA, writing a dissertation on the prohibition movement in California, and taught history at Upland College, a small college associated with the Brethren in Christ, until that college closed for financial reasons in 1963 and merged with Messiah College in Pennsylvania. After Upland closed, Harmon taught at Mt. San Antonio Community College until retirement.

Many COs were frustrated by their Forest Service work. Not only did it not seem to be "work of national importance," it also failed to make use of their talents and education. Men with college degrees were building stone walls or felling snags; men who had grown up as farmers were building roads or fire lookout towers at a time when agricultural labor was in short supply. An alternative that had been identified by Selective Service was work in hospitals, particularly mental hospitals. As more and more men entered the military and the supply of labor decreased, it became difficult to recruit workers for low-paying jobs such as hospital attendants. War-related industries were paying premium wages. During the spring of 1942, Mark Schrock began to investigate possibilities for such "detached service" in mental hospitals for the men of CPS #21. In May, Schrock and three campers, Alan McRae, George Wells and Charlie Davis, made an all-day visit to the Oregon State mental hospital in Salem to explore the possibility of establishing a detached unit there. Up to forty men could be assigned there to work with the patients in the wards as attendants, to work in the laboratory, and to do supervisory work on the farm associated with the hospital. Two other hospital units were also under consideration: Eastern Oregon State Hospital at Pendleton and Western State Hospital at Fort Steilacoom, WA.[2]

The Salem hospital project ran into local opposition. The board of the Salem Trade and Labor council failed to recommend that the CO unit be formed, even though a letter had been sent assuring the council that the men were eager to cooperate with labor. Apparently, the council feared that having unpaid COs at the hospital would perpetuate poor labor conditions. The local American Legion also protested the formation of the unit, even though conferences were held to inform the members of the Legion of the serious labor shortages at the hospital. The protests appear to have been precipitated by the news that Salem's Willamette University President Carl Sumner Knopf had registered with Selective Service as a conscientious objector.[3] The Salem and Pendleton units were never formed, but a group of CPS #21 men went to Fort Steilacoom in September 1942 to establish a permanent CPS unit (CPS #51).

By spring of 1942, the Wyeth camp was organized and running smoothly, and special interest groups began to form. Many men at Cascade Locks, more than thirty according to *The Columbian*, were members of the Fellowship of Reconciliation (FOR), perhaps the largest pacifist organization in the United States, led by A. J. Muste. The FOR had been founded in England in December 1914 by a group of Christian pacifists "profoundly dissatisfied by the confused utterance of the Christian churches concerning the war." The American branch was established in November 1915. After World War I FOR had established itself as the leading voice for pacifism in the U.S.[4] In May the CPS #21 members of FOR came together to form a local chapter in the camp with George Brown, a recent arrival from Los Angeles, as chairman, and Philip Isely, another recent arrival from Salem, Oregon, as secretary. They developed a program that focused on an "analysis of life programs (with particular attention to vocations) which each member hopes to carry out to determine the most effective methods of working for a peaceful and cooperative society."[5]

At the same time a camp local of the Socialist Party was organized with George S. Wells as chair and Bill Webb as secretary. The Socialists were an outspoken group. In late May they sent an appeal to other CPS camps and pacifist groups to support a Socialist move toward an immediate peace offensive. Their policy statement read:

> *We believe that the United States is waging a war for the defense and extension of imperialistic commerce and for the perpetuation of vested interests in financial and political power – rather than for freedom democracy and political power.*
>
> *Because of these underlying motives and because of our belief that armed conflict can never achieve correction of social ills, we urge the party to withhold support of the war and to initiate immediately a peace offensive directed toward establishment of a foundation for a cooperative classless society.*
>
> *We urge that the Party direct its energies toward control of the government through legal and peaceful channels and an educational program. Socialists must strive to direct the current trend of economic planning toward a democratic collectivism. The full-capacity mobilization of men, materials and machinery must be turned away from war production to the satisfaction of human needs.*
>
> *Immediate pressure must be brought to bear upon the government to preserve such fundamental democratic principles as the preservation of civil liberties – speech, press, religion and public assembly; racial and minority tolerance; the right of self-determination for the soldier, laborer, and conscientious objector.*[6]

This statement created quite a stir. On June 3, Harold Row wrote to Mark Schrock indicating that Row had received "several kick backs from our Camp Directors over the material sent to the various camps by the Cascade Locks Socialist Party." While recognizing the freedom of speech issues involved and assuring Schrock that he was not giving him a direct order, Row went on to express his opinion that "such activities should be curbed in the right way. Our camp directors do not want such activities initiated in their camps and I am sure that such circulars would cause considerable difficulties with Selective Service, and the general public if they knew about it. I would be happy if such activities could be discontinued both in the camps and between the camps."[7]

Mark Schrock wrote back on June 10 to apologize for the disturbance and to assure Row that "we are trying to work with the fellows involved and with our public relations committee in the camp for a quieting of this problem, if not the complete removal." He encouraged Row to have the offended camps write directly to the men, rather than approaching the problem indirectly.[8] In his memoir Julian Schrock suggests that his father was probably quite sympathetic to the socialists. Apparently, Mark Schrock twice voted for Norman Thomas, the Socialist candidate for president, and was very active in the cooperative movement, both in Olympia before the war and after his return to Indiana in 1944. He did not hide the fact that he disliked capitalism.[9] But Schrock understood the difficulty for CPS, with the public and Congress unsympathetic to COs, and an authoritarian mentality at Selective Service. Within a month he would relearn these lessons in an even more dramatic way.

As summer approached, the Forest Service opened two new side camps: one at Lost Lake and another at Mud Lake. Side camps were established for any significant work project too far from the Wyeth camp for transporting men back and forth each day. Side camps also provided faster response to forest fires, because crews were dispersed around the Mt. Hood National Forest. The Lost Lake camp housed about fifty men who undertook road, trail, and forest fire prevention work. They slept in tents, but the other camp facilities, such as the mess hall and showers, were housed in temporary buildings. Each side camp was supervised by a Forest Service representative and an assignee leader who took care of all the camp administrative details. The leader of the Lost Lake camp was Bob Case, a Presbyterian from Oakland, California, who eventually served as co-director of the Wyeth camp. Depending on the size of the side camp, several campers would also be assigned to overhead jobs such as cook, KP, and night watchman.

The Mud Lake camp, located on the saddle of a windy ridge a few miles from Wahtum Lake, was smaller. Eleven men were assigned

Lost Lake side camp where the COs slept in tents. (*LC Sheets 4:S54*)

there for three weeks to work on trails and roads. The men lived in an old warehouse that had been divided into three rooms. Water was carried in from a spring. Although the living conditions were primitive, the views of Mount Hood, Mount St. Helens, Mount Adams, and even Mount Rainier, over one hundred miles to the north, were magnificent.[10]

In June, ninety-eight men at the Wyeth camp made a plea to the Governor of Virginia, Colgate W. Darden, Jr., to commute the death sentence of an African-American sharecropper, Odell Waller. Waller had been convicted of murdering his white landlord, but the Workers Defense League, which had taken up Waller's appeal, claimed that he had acted in self-defense and that the jury-selection process was biased. The case was brought to the camp's attention by assignee Paul Holtzman. Camp public relations director Richard Mills phoned the Governor and learned that Waller had been given a ten-day reprieve while the case was investigated,[11] but the plea proved unsuccessful and Waller died in the electric chair of the Virginia State Penitentiary on July 2, 1942.[12]

When the camp government was established, terms of office had been set at four months, so new elections were held for officers who would take over on July 1. Charlie Davis won the race for camp president. Davis was originally from Oklahoma City but had attended the University of Southern California where he played in the Trojan Band and earned a degree in accounting. After graduation he was a civilian employee for the United States Navy. Despite assurances that

Special occasion in the dining hall. Charlie Davis is standing in the foreground addressing the diners. Dick Mills, assistant director, is seated next to Davis on the right in the photo. (*LC Schrock 23*)

George Yamada, William McReynolds and Alden Douglas working in the Wyeth kitchen. (*LC Blocher D12*)

if he remained with the Navy he would not see combat, Davis applied for and was awarded the 4-E classification and was one of the large group of Californians who had arrived at Cascade Locks on December 5, 1941. Davis quickly became a camp leader because of his intelligence, personal charisma, managerial skills, and quick wit that could defuse a difficult situation. All his abilities were required to help manage the situation that the camp faced as he assumed office: the order from Selective Service to remove George Yamada.

The Yamada Protest

George Kiyoshi Yamada had also arrived at Cascade Locks on December 5, 1941 with the large contingent from California. He was born in 1918 just outside the small town of Minatare, a sugar beet farming community in western Nebraska. When Yamada's father had refused to be conscripted into the armed forces of Japan, which was preparing for a war with Russia, the family had emigrated to the United States a few years before his birth. Although Yamada's parents were devoted Methodist converts, he had ceased attending church at age twelve because he felt that the church fell short in its application of Christian teachings in daily life. He had become a firm pacifist, however. At age nineteen he moved to San Francisco, became part of the local Nisei community, and eventually began to attend San Francisco State College, where he majored in journalism. Yamada was awarded the 4-E classification by his local Selective Service board in the fall of 1941 and received orders to report to CPS Camp #21.[13]

Yamada was one of the first men assigned to the Larch Mountain side camp, where he was elected to the education committee. After proclamations by President Roosevelt shortly after Pearl Harbor declared all nationals and subjects of Japan, Germany and Italy as alien enemies and permitted the Department of Justice summarily to apprehend any such persons who were deemed "dangerous to the public peace or safety of the United States,"[14] Yamada decided that it would be best for him not to be away from camp on work projects, so he voluntarily became part of the camp overhead and worked as a cook at Larch Mountain and eventually at the main camp at Wyeth. Although Roosevelt's statements had also included Germans and Italians, Lt. General John L. DeWitt, the commanding officer of the Western Defense Command (WDC), based in the Presidio in San Francisco, was focused on the threat from the Japanese. Finding the justice department efforts inadequate, he pushed for military involvement. His "Final Recommendation," issued in February 1942, stated:

In the war in which we are now engaged racial identities are not severed by migration. The Japanese race is an enemy race and while many second and third generation Japanese born on United States soil, possessed of United States citizenship, have become "Americanized," the racial strains are undiluted . . . . It therefore follows that along the vital Pacific Coast over 112,000 potential enemies are at large today.[15]

This recommendation helped persuade President Franklin Roosevelt to issue Executive Order 9066, signed on February 19, 1942, authorizing the removal of persons of Japanese descent from most of the west coast. This order and the subsequent enabling legislation led to the removal and incarceration of these 112,000 "potential enemies" in what amounted to concentration camps surrounded by barbed wire and located in remote places, although none of the approximately 114,000 persons of Italian descent or 97,000 persons of German descent living in the restricted zone were included in the mass removal.[16]

Although CPS camps were not surrounded by barbed wire patrolled by armed guards, the COs were under the tight control of the Selective Service system. The policy of Selective Service concerning those men assigned to Civilian Public Service, was described by Lieutenant Colonel Franklin L. McLean of the Camp Operations Division:

From the time an assignee reports to camp until he is finally released he is under the control of the Director of Selective Service. He ceases to be a free agent and is accountable for all of his time, in camp and out, 24 hours a day. His movement, actions and conduct are subject to control and regulation. He ceases to have certain rights and is granted privileges instead. These privileges can be restricted or withdrawn without his consent as punishment, during emergency or as a matter of policy. He may be told when and how to work, what to wear and where to sleep. He can be required to submit to medical examinations and treatment, and to practice rules of health and sanitation. He may be moved from place to place and from job to job, even to foreign countries, for the convenience of the government regardless of his personal feelings or desires.[17]

Under these circumstances it may be difficult to understand why the Wartime Civil Control Administration, directed by Colonel Karl R. Bendetsen, who was the architect of the Japanese removal and incarceration, decided that Yamada, a citizen of Japanese ancestry, should be discharged from confinement at Cascade Locks and interned in a relocation facility operated by the War Relocation Authority. The order from Camp Operations Division of Selective Service was sent in a telegram to Mark Schrock:

> *George Kiyoshi Yamada is to be discharged from CPS Camp No.21 Cascade Locks, Oregon, in order that he may be sent to a camp under the jurisdiction of the War Relocation Authority. This man is to be discharged upon receipt by the Camp Director of information from the Office of the Commanding General, Headquarters Western Defense Command and Fourth Army, Presidio of San Francisco, California.[18]*

Under the peculiar arrangements between Selective Service and the Historic Peace Churches, Mark Schrock was an employee of the Brethren Service Committee but directly responsible to the officers of the Selective Service System. After talking with George Yamada and others, Schrock responded with a letter to General Hershey and Colonel Kosch. Copies, or similar letters, were sent to Paul Comly French and to W. Harold Row, the Director of Civilian Public Service for the Brethren Service Committee. The letters were dated June 30, 1942.[19] After some background information concerning his own involvement with CPS and about George Yamada's history and character, Schrock continues:

> *When the authorization was made known to our men they were deeply moved with a sense of injustice and decided to raise a protest directly. This they did in the night letter, copy of which is enclosed, which they sent to Selective Service. I have not yet informed the boys in our camp regarding my own relationship to the affair, but I shall of course do it soon.*
>
> *With my present light I cannot conscientiously sign my name to the discharge papers nor to the government requests for transportation, meals, and lodging, because by so doing I become for one short moment a part of the administration of the ruthless treatment of a part of humanity and discrimination and punishment of our own fellow citizens by the United States government. This I cannot do, although I am now as eager as ever to give of my time and energy to any constructive work that can be done for the well being of my country as a whole without inflicting injustice or participating in what fair minded men of today and all future ages must see as a crime and an insane inhumanity to man.*

*I do not know what such inability to cooperate on this will involve.
I do not know whether you and the Brethren Service Committee will
consider my stand to be in accordance with the Christian values and
your desires or not. If you do share with me in my position, I shall
welcome your suggestions on procedure. You may even wish to negotiate
with Selective Service and NSBRO for a stay in the order for discharge,
and if necessary for the transfer of this assignee to some CPS camp not in
the area of evacuation. I would be perfectly willing to sign transportation
and meal and lodging requests should it be desired that this assignee
should be transferred to another CPS camp farther inland.*

*If you do not share my attitude you may consider this as my
resignation as director of CPS camp 21, and if you wish to avoid
making any open issue of this case, you may wire your acceptance of
my resignation effective immediately. You will then be free to appoint
someone else as director or acting director to care for this matter without
incident or delay.*

*P. S. This letter has been read to the entire staff of our camp and they
have with one accord expressed their agreement in the position indicated
and their unwillingness to sign the papers involved. This is merely for
your information.*

On June 29 Schrock discussed the situation in a formal meeting
of the nearly two hundred men then living in the camp. A second
meeting was held the following day at which nonviolent techniques
were discussed.[20] As Kermit Sheets, a member of the camp at the time,
remembered,

*And wow, that camp blew apart! Because here was a guy as isolated
as you could be. We knew George, he was a conscientious objector, for
crying out loud! He wasn't going to send messages to Japan that would
make them shoot us! The whole thing was absolutely ridiculous. Then
we had loads of meetings as to how we were going to handle it when they
came for George. It got extremely tense, verging on the melodramatic, for
the feelings that were there. People wondering how many people should
lie down in front of the car that was to take him away.[21]*

George Brown thought he had a wonderful idea, which was to
kidnap Yamada when the authorities came for him. This scheme would
arouse national interest in the whole affair and force a Congressional
investigation of the Japanese relocation. He even had a confession

of kidnapping all written out for anyone interested to sign.[22] This suggestion was taken seriously enough that on July 3 Mark Schrock and Dick Mills consulted a lawyer in Portland concerning the legal aspects of the Yamada case, including the kidnapping possibility.[23]

Eventually a telegram was drafted and sent to General Hershey, and a letter including the text of the telegram sent to the other forty CPS camps across the country, where some 3,500 objectors were then serving.[24] This letter, also dated June 30, 1942, was prepared by a committee, but signed by Camp President Charlie Davis on behalf of the camp.[25] The letter opened with a description of the situation including the text of the order to discharge Yamada. Following this background the letter continued:

> *George has won the respect of every member of the camp for his honesty and integrity, and the reaction was one of approval when he told them that he would not accept evacuation.*
>
> *The 200-odd men who comprise this camp are agreed in a philosophy opposed to race discrimination. Because of our basic belief in full racial equality and our objection to restriction of civil liberties, we have sent the following telegram to Selective Service, and have written similar letters to N. S. B. R. O., Forest Service, and other interested agencies:"Feeling great injustice in the evacuation of fellow citizens of Japanese ancestry, enjoying the same constitutional rights that we enjoy, we strongly urge the rescinding of the discharge order affecting George Yamada of C. P. S. Camp 21." What the reaction of Selective Service will be, may only be surmised. But there is no basis in the past treatment of Japanese Americans, on which to assume that our request for rescinding of the discharge order will be readily granted. Since we regard George Yamada as our equal and ourselves as no more nor less than he, we are prepared to take non-violent direct action appropriate to the response we receive from Selective Service. (A hunger strike, a work strike, non-violent resistance to his removal from the camp, or insistence upon sharing whatever treatment is accorded him, have been suggested as possible courses of action.)*
>
> *In view of the fact that speed is imperative, may we suggest that you take the matter under discussion upon receipt of this letter and let us know by the quickest method the immediate result of your meeting.*
>
> *We would be happy to have your support in what we consider a Christian undertaking. Your letters or telegrams to Selective Service*

*and the War Relocation Authority will add weight to the appeal we have
made. We also welcome your suggestions for further action, and your
comments on the action already taken.*

Similar letters were sent to ministers and leaders of organizations
thought to be interested in civil liberties issues. A letter was sent to
Milton Eisenhower, then the Director of the War Relocation Authority
(WRA). In the spirit of openness essential to Gandhian non-violent
direct action, copies were sent to Selective Service and the WDC. No
copies were sent to the press and there was no press notice of the
confrontation. Gandhian thought was important to many COs who
used his philosophy as the basis of their resistance to war and, in
some cases to conscription. For others, particularly the Mennonites,
Gandhian techniques were purely political and had no place in their
philosophy of non-resistance. The leaders of the Yamada protest were
sympathetic to Gandhian philosophy and techniques.[26]

Response to the letter was prompt, with strong support by telegram
from the camp in Coshocton, Ohio, (CPS #23): "Feeling deep concern
over discharge order affecting George Yamada and aware of the
fellowship which is our strength. We pledge to follow your lead in
non-violent direct action if necessary." The Petersham, Massachusetts,
camp (CPS #9) wrote: "Camp much interested in Yamada case. Taking
action by wire and letter as explained in air mail letter following. Please
keep us advised of developments." The Royalston, Massachusetts,
camp wrote, "If it is possible, we would like Mr. Yamada to become
member of CPS #10, Royalston." Similar support came from at least
two other camps (#19 in Marion, NC, and #37 in Coleville, California),
from national pacifist organizations, and from prominent individuals
including A. J. Muste of the Fellowship of Reconciliation.[27]

In a ten-page report on the Yamada incident, public relations director
and camp staff member Richard Mills summarized and analyzed the
responses. The largest number of positive responses came from Friends
camps. Thoughtful responses were received from three Brethren camps,
but the opinion was highly divided. The camp at Walhalla was strongly
supportive, but the other two camps were more conservative. The
Mennonite camps responded with the accepted Mennonite philosophy
of non-resistance, and generally suggested taking the matter to God
in prayer. The responses from "interested friends," as Mills termed
them, was similarly divided, ranging from the strong support of A. J.

Muste, Executive Director of the Fellowship of Reconciliation, to more critical responses from prominent pacifists Arthur E. Morgan, former President of Antioch College and the first director of the Tennessee Valley Authority, and Oswald Garrison Villard, former editor of the *Nation*, who were concerned that non-violent direct action could bring down the entire CPS system by angering both the public and the government.[28]

Although there was broad agreement concerning the injustice of the Japanese removal and incarceration, a significant minority of the campers did not support non-violent direct action in resistance to the order. Forty-eight men who believed in non-resistance signed the following letter to Colonel Kosch:[29]

> *We, the undersigned of C. P. S. Camp #21, are hereby giving our statement to clarify our stand in regard to the action taken by the camp concerning the evacuation of George Yamada. We feel that the Japanese evacuation order is wholly wrong and wish to state that we agree with our camp in principle, but not in the method of action taken.*
>
> *We as Christians, adhering to the privilege granted to us by our Government and placing ourselves totally in the grace of God, cannot sanction any method of non-violent direct action. Therefore, we want it clearly understood that we played no part therein. We believe that the powers that be are ordained of God and it is our sincere desire to cooperate with our government in any way we can without violating our conscience. We thank God that we have the privilege of being in service to our country in a C. P. S. Camp.*
>
> *In conclusion, let us make it known that we desire and are striving for camp unity and hope that a repetition of disagreements does not occur.*

This disagreement concerning tactics shows the deep philosophical differences among the COs concerning their relationship with the government.[30] A significant fraction of men in CPS, including many Mennonites, followed what Grimsrud called the "servant tendency," and deferred to government authority, which they regarded as ordained by God. As the letter to Kosch disagreeing with the use of non-violent direct action makes clear, for them alternative service was a privilege and an opportunity to show their faith and in some cases their patriotism. They believed it was their Christian duty to obey the state in all requirements that did not violate the teachings of God. Many Quakers, on the other hand, did not feel any compulsion to obey the state. Quakers believed that the true and right were to be discovered in the inner light burning in each individual. If the state required something that contradicted the dictates of conscience, then the individual had a moral obligation to speak out or to combat what was wrong. This position was shared, at least in spirit, by those COs of other religious or philosophical persuasions who were motivated by a strong sense of social justice. Often they were so articulate and active that they became the leaders in the camps, startling those who came merely to abstain from the war. These were Grimsrud's "transformers." This tension, found in many CPS camps, is clearly shown by the contrast between the two letters quoted above.[31] Between these two extremes were the Brethren, who took a position of conciliation. The Brethren were not bound by creedal obligation to obey the state, but they recognized that total rejection of government leads to anarchy. The Brethren leadership regarded CPS as an appropriate compromise and worked to mediate disagreements.

On June 29, 1942, when Yamada was told he would be discharged by Selective Service "in order that he may be sent to a camp under the jurisdiction of the War Relocation Authority," all other persons of Japanese ancestry, some one hundred thousand citizens and long-term resident aliens, had been removed from the western parts of California, Oregon and Washington to assembly centers, awaiting transfer to detention camps. There was very little protest of the Japanese removal, nor was there much resistance. Senator Sheridan Downey of California and Congressmen Jerry Voorhies and John Coffee vocally opposed the removal program. The Mayor of Tacoma, Washington, Harry Cain, also publicly protested, but there was virtually no open opposition from church leaders.[32] In fact, there was strong support for the removal throughout the country. A few Japanese showed enormous courage in challenging the order. Minoru Yasui, a native of Hood River, had violated curfew and had been tried in Portland on June 12, 1942. Gordon Hirabayashi, a Quaker who had been classified 4-E, was scheduled to leave for CPS Camp #21 on April 23, 1942, but that order was canceled the day before, so he remained in Seattle. Hirabayashi, a student at the University of Washington, had violated curfew and refused to report for removal in May and was awaiting trial in Seattle. A third Japanese-American, Fred Korematsu, had been apprehended in San Leandro, California, for violating the removal order and retained a lawyer to challenge the order.[33]

Meanwhile, Colonel Kosch was said to be very disturbed with the protest and was certain that the men in the camp had been plotting against the government for a long time. He was ready to fly out to Oregon to take over the Wyeth camp himself.[34] In Washington, the executive secretary of the NSBRO advised the BSC that he was doing everything possible to keep Yamada at Cascade Locks. Paul Comly French's diary for July 3, 1942 indicates that telegrams and letters of protest were arriving at Selective Service, and that Orie Miller, CPS director for the Mennonite Central Committee, reported that even the normally placid Mennonite camps were disturbed over the Yamada situation. On July 4, 1942, French reported a breakthrough: "Called Colonel Karl Bendetsen in San Francisco today and talked to him about the Yamada case at Cascade Locks. He agreed to issue a travel permit to allow us to move him to another camp in the interior rather than send him to a reception center. He was very friendly on the phone and it looks like the luncheons and visits of several months ago bore fruit."[35] Mark Schrock informed the camp at noon on July 4 that he had received a call from French indicating that the government had rescinded the removal order, and that Yamada would be able to transfer to another CPS camp outside the restricted zone.[36]

French's diary entry indicates that one reason Bendetsen agreed to his request was the personal relationship between them. One possible factor is that Bendetsen had earlier opposed General DeWitt's proclamation imposing a curfew and travel restrictions on all persons of Japanese descent. Bendetsen felt that there should have been provision for exceptions in special cases. He might have felt that Yamada was one of those exceptions. A second possible factor was the sensitivity of Bendetsen and all others involved with the Japanese removal and incarceration to adverse press. Bendetsen briefed the press in the principal cities along the West Coast about the removal process and asked them to avoid exacerbating what was already a tense situation.[37] The Selective Service was similarly sensitive to bad publicity, so Bendetsen may have seen the transfer of George Yamada to an inland camp as a convenient solution to a potential public relations nightmare.[38]

Kosch did not come to Cascade Locks, but W. Harold Row, director of Civilian Public Service for the Brethren Service Committee, did come on July 6 and expressed the displeasure of Selective Service, NSBRO, and the Brethren Service Committee concerning the protest. Row emphasized both the fragility of the agreement between the churches and Selective Service, and that the men were subject to the very strict rules that Selective Service had promulgated. Apparently, Kosch was sufficiently upset to suggest the whole CPS program would be in danger if the men got too out of hand.[39] He repeated the government and army position that the Japanese were not being mistreated but rather protected by the removal. Row was also upset because the men had taken direct action in writing to General Hershey rather than going through the channels of authority.[40]

Caught in the middle between the Selective Service with its military mentality and complete power over the COs and the young idealists at Cascade Locks, Harold Row was trying to preserve the CPS system, which in spite of its shortcomings was an improvement over the situation COs endured during World War I. Row was a Church of the Brethren minister, and his personal position seems to have been closer to the non-resisters at Cascade Locks than to the activists. His remarks on July 6 referred to going the "second mile." This command derives from the Sermon on the Mount in *Matthew* 5:41. It epitomized the service philosophy of many in the Historic Peace Churches, particularly the Mennonites and Brethren. They believed that the testimony of love could be expressed even within the framework of conscription. If compelled to go one mile, the non-resistant Christian is willing to go a second mile voluntarily.

Harold Row was also a representative of the Brethren Service Committee. The official goals of the Brethren CPS camps included offering "a medium for the preservation and continued expression of our own and other Christian bodies," and assisting the "government in developing appropriate measures by which religious minorities which conscientiously reject military service may bear witness in times of war in a manner consistent with the principles of religious liberty and the priority of individual rights which a democratic government must guarantee."[41] This doctrine may explain why Mark Schrock, also a Church of the Brethren minister, took such a courageous and risky stand. Those who knew him describe Schrock as a man of principle who stood firm when he felt he was right.[42] It is probably significant that Schrock knew some Japanese-Americans personally. Before coming to Cascade Locks, Schrock had lived in Olympia, where his family was friendly with a Japanese family, the Taharas, who later were forced to move to the Tule Lake Relocation Center. Schrock did his best to help the Taharas, and on one occasion his family visited their friends at Tule Lake.[43] Schrock also had strong support from the men in the camp, including some thoughtful and articulate leaders with whom he was very close: J. Henry Dasenbrock, Charlie Davis, and George Brown. Diary entries report that after Row's remarks, Schrock apologized for not having gone through the appropriate channels, but stated that he felt that the removal order was unjust and that he would resign before doing what he thought was wrong. Schrock took the path of conscience, which was the way he lived his life.

One of the results of Row's four-day visit to Cascade Locks was that Charlie Davis did write a conciliatory letter to Colonel Kosch in which he admitted there were "several points of weakness" in their action. These included their failure first to send Selective Service copies of their communications to other camps and individuals; and second, to try to work with Selective Service to find a solution before going to other camps and friends. Finally, Davis insisted that the action was not intended to challenge the authority of Selective Service, but to protest the "removal of our Japanese American friend and the principle of evacuation based on race." The letter also explained what the COs meant by non-violent direct action, and emphasized that their action was based on a feeling of injustice and was not directed at any individual. Although the tone of the letter is conciliatory, it ends with a strong statement of principle:

> *In the days ahead we seek the courage to stand for the right as we see it and the wisdom to act on behalf of the right fearlessly. And in so doing, we recognize the importance of being sure, as long as we are in camp, that the issues which arouse our concern and conviction are made clear to all administrative agencies connected with the camp. We trust and believe, that in the future when social issues are of concern to us, that our relations with Selective Service and the administrative agencies will proceed in a friendly manner.*[44]

Yamada agreed to accept a transfer to an inland CPS camp. A letter was prepared and sent to all CPS camps and other interested persons. It contained the following statement from George Yamada clarifying his position:

> *I believe that the principle of evacuation of any people on the ground of race alone is a great wrong, both morally and socially. I want to state*

here a feeling of admiration and respect for Gordon Hirabayashi and the stand which he has taken in opposition to this principle. I feel that I have a great moral responsibility to oppose any such measure which violates this principle. Believing that some of you may wish to continue your protest against the whole principle of evacuation, not just in my case alone, I wish it clearly understood that I leave CPS #21 only under severe pressure of circumstances.

In accepting this transfer order to an inland CPS camp I am frankly admitting a weakness. I feel that I am not strong enough to face the issue uncompromisingly. I wish to make it clear that I have never expressed a willingness to be transferred from this area. I have stated that I would accept such a transfer, but I have not desired it. Often our words do not express our true motives but rather confuse them, as mine to the National Service Board apparently has done in this case.

In compliance with the order I am giving to Mark Schrock my preference for a transfer to some midwestern or eastern camp. I appreciate the support and backing which the fellows have given me in a matter not concerning themselves personally. When I leave I will always carry with me a sense of pride and humility at having had the opportunity to have been a part of this group, here and at Larch Mountain.[45]

In addition, the letter asked for support for Gordon Hirabayashi, then awaiting trial in Seattle.

George Yamada received travel authorization from the WDC and transfer approval from Selective Service for a move to CPS Camp #5 at Colorado Springs, Colorado. He left Cascade Locks on July 26, 1942. He spent several years at Colorado Springs. Shortly after his arrival he reported to Mark and Mabel Schrock on his new situation. He compared life at CPS #5 unfavorably to that at CPS #21 and indicated he had been assigned to the dishwashing crew where he was "putting in 8 hours of socially significant labor."[46] At CPS #5 he became increasingly politically active. In the Grimsrud typology, he became a "resister." Near the end of his time there, when he participated in a project of the Congress of Racial Equality to desegregate the local theaters, he was arrested and spent eight days in the El Paso County Jail. Through the efforts of his attorney he was transferred to the Government-operated CPS camp at Germfask, Michigan. After less than six months in this camp, he "walked out" in defiance of the Selective Service Act and was sentenced to three and a half years in prison. He served time in the Federal Prison in Ashland, Kentucky, where he participated in an action organized by Bayard Rustin to desegregate the dining hall. As a result of that action he was transferred to Danbury, Connecticut, where he served additional time until his release in 1946. Like many COs, he did not serve his full sentence.[47]

While not a satisfactory repudiation of the government's removal and incarceration program, the confrontation at the Locks brought a unique reversal of a decision of the WDC and stands in history as one of the few national protests of the removal. In retrospect, it is noteworthy that a principled action by a small group of men forced the War Relocation Authority to back down, albeit in a small matter. Perhaps if others, particularly the churches, had raised a major public protest, General DeWitt's plan would not have been carried out.

One of the objectives of the Brethren CPS program was "to demonstrate and extend the spirit of brotherhood and justice as a way of life which leads to world-mindedness and to international peace and security."[48] In responding to the order to evacuate George Yamada, the men of CPS #21 showed that at their best the COs exemplified this ideal. Their protest challenged the arbitrary authority of both the Selective Service System and the Western Defense Command, and resulted in a small moment of justice in one of the great injustices in American history.

Opening of Fort Steilacoom and Waldport

Following the departure of George Yamada, two other groups of men left Cascade Locks. The detached service unit at Fort Steilacoom was finally organized, and fifteen men led by Charlie Davis traveled there in September. Among them were former Camp President Bill Phillips, Al Hastings, who had organized the camp chorus, and flautist Windsor Utley. The Fort Steilacoom unit became CPS Camp #51 and remained open until October 1945. Some of the men worked as attendants, but others held different jobs. Bill Cable was a truck driver; Henry Carlsen worked in the hospital kitchen; and Loyd Schaad, who had earned an M.S. in horticulture, managed the hospital grounds. Henry Blocher became the hospital photographer. The project began with the full support of the governor of Washington, Arthur B. Langlie, who wrote to General Hershey, "Therefore, I wish it to be known that the plan to use religious objectors in our public institutions has the support of this administration and insofar as we are able to ascertain, of all other interested agencies."[49] Another ten men transferred to the new BSC camp #56 at Waldport, Oregon. This camp, also known as Camp Angel, was about a block and a half from the ocean. As Northwest supervisor for Brethren camps, Mark Schrock had oversight responsibilities for both new camps, and close connections were maintained among the three units throughout the war.

After the war Windsor Utley began to develop his talent for painting, influenced by Mark Tobey, one of the founders of the Northwest School located in Skagit County, Washington.[50] Utley became an award-winning artist, head of the art department at the Cornish College of the Arts in Seattle and the owner of galleries in Seattle, Sydney, British Columbia, and Laguna Beach, California. Although Utley was known primarily as an artist, he maintained his interest in the flute, continuing to teach and perform throughout his life.[51]

There were also administrative changes at CPS #21 during the summer. Richard Mills, an assignee from Los Angeles, who had been a YMCA Secretary and public relations director at the camp, was appointed assistant director. At age thirty-four Mills was older than

Les Abbenhouse, Maud Gregory, Richard Anderson, Mark Schrock, Lewey Newmann, Gilbert Grover and Jack Mulkey relaxing on the lawn at CPS #21. (*Brethren*)

most of the campers, had earned a master's degree from Columbia University, and had considerable administrative and personnel experience. Mark Schrock identified him as an excellent candidate almost immediately and wrote to Harold Row suggesting that Mills be appointed as assistant director. Because Mennonites and Brethren were a minority of the camp population, Schrock wanted to broaden the composition of the administrative staff.[52] Because of his teaching background Albert Bohrer took over as education director until his transfer to the Mennonite CPS camp at North Fork, California in August.[53] In September, George Brown was elected education director, the first staff member to be chosen by the assignees. Brown defeated Kermit Sheets in a very close election. Election of the education director was a way to include camp members more directly in camp decision-making. The democratic decision-making processes were tested again in September and October when another controversy arose, this time involving what many men thought was a war-related work project.

The Three Lynx Protest

At the end of September 1942 the Forest Service approached Mark Schrock with a plan to open a new side camp on the Clackamas River near Estacada, Oregon, where eighty CPS men would work with about fifty Forest Service employees to build new logging roads into the largest tract of virgin timber in the United States. This proposed camp was named Three Lynx. As Schrock explained in an airmail letter to Harold Row dated October 2, 1942, this project would last for twelve to eighteen months, and would require a virtually self-sufficient camp because it was located nearly a hundred miles from Wyeth. The Forest Service had offered to provide $1.50 per day for food for the men on the project, which was three to four times as much as the food budget at Cascade Locks. Schrock's letter went on to discuss some administrative matters, including the question of who should be sent to the new camp as an assistant director and various financial considerations.

At first glance this matter seems straightforward, but Shrock's letter includes a sentence foreshadowing a controversy that occupied the camp for the next month and a half, and eventually involved the leadership of Brethren CPS and Paul Comly French in discussions with both the Forest Service and the Selective Service in Washington. On page two of a three-page letter, Schrock writes in his typical understated prose, "There seems to be some misgivings on the part of some of the men of our camp as to how closely the opening up of these roads into that new source of lumber is geared into the entire national defense program." Although James Frankland, the regional engineer for the Forest Service, had assured Mark Schrock that opening up this stand of timber was a project that had been planned before the war had started, Schrock requested that Frankland or someone from his office come to Cascade Locks to explain the whole matter to the men.

The misgivings of the men at Cascade Locks were fueled by articles about the proposed project that appeared in both the *Oregonian* and the *Oregon Journal*, the two Portland dailies, over the next several days. On October 4, the *Oregonian* reported that "announcement was made of allocating $250,000 for road improvement and sale of additional tract of timber by Dwyer Bros. Logging Company." The *Oregon Journal* carried a story that "some 500 West Coast lumbermen were notified at a meeting at Hotel Portland Tuesday they shortly will have but one customer—the United States Government." A new government order was to become effective on October 29, after which "all Douglas fir must be directed to government needs. The army-navy procurement office here will make all the purchases." A letter to the camp from J. J. Handsaker of the National Council for the Prevention of War advised that "no roads are being built that do not have direct relation to winning the war."[54]

Frankland did come to Cascade Locks, with Jack Horton from the Regional Office of the Forest Service. The discussion was recorded and a nine-page summary dated October 7, 1942 was prepared.[55] Frankland and Horton were open and honest. Their introductory remarks noted that the purpose of the Forest Service was more than growing trees; the forests were there to provide a livelihood for as many people as possible. Plans for development of the Clackamas River area dated back as far as 1933 when the CCC began to build roads into it, but the work had not been finished. Now that money was available, they wanted to complete the work. Frankland commented, "The thing in your minds is, 'in what way is that project connected with the war effort?' Well, not much that the Forest Service is doing at present is not connected with the war effort." But he added, "We do not consider this definitely a war effort but part of a Forest Service development in the developing of this particular area to the point where it will provide its maximum amount of employment annually." When asked why CPS men were being asked to work on this project, Frankland pointed out that there was a labor shortage. His preference was to use ordinary labor, but he couldn't find it and was turning to CPS.

The questions and statements from the COs focused on the direct relationship of the project with the war and the problem of conscience. The reason they were in CPS was to do constructive work for the country that did not contribute directly to the war. They were happy to do conservation work, for example, but the Three Lynx project seemed to many to be directly connected to the war effort. Both Frankland and Horton seemed sympathetic. For example, in response to a question as to whether the Forest Service felt that the CPS men should do any work assigned to them, one of them said, "There are things which we will not ask you to do." Horton is quoted as saying, "I am more interested in people than I am in trees or anything else. . . . We are going to try to get those jobs done without any fight. We are not going to fight, not even verbally, if we can help it." The meeting may have cleared the air, but it did not settle the matter. At the end some men firmly opposed participation in the project, others were willing to cooperate, and of course some were undecided.

Twelve men were sent to Three Lynx as a temporary crew in early October.[56] Their initial task was to construct the buildings for the new camp. A crew under the direction of Bob Case remained at Three Lynx until December.[57] The debate continued. The October 1942 issue of the

The controversial Three Lynx camp under construction. (*Brethren*)

Columbian contained two opinion pieces in response to the question, "Would you work on the road project at Estacada?" one yes and one no. Bill Finley, who said yes because the road was needed and would be of lasting value after the war, added that he would "oppose our being *forced* to accept it as a project." Wilmer Carlson, who said no, gave as his reason that the timber would be used for war purposes and contributing to the war effort was something he would not do. Eighty-six men signed a petition indicating that they would refuse to work on the Three Lynx project for reasons of conscience.[58]

Some men went further. Joe Gunterman sent a letter to Paul Comly French, which was also signed by four other men (Douglas Strain, Ralph Soelzer, Windsor Utley and Nathan Barad), on October 13. Gunterman's letter is worth quoting in full:

> I understand that a number of our men have written you in opposition to the new side camp for CPS 21 which is to be located on the Clackamas River near Estacada, Oregon. I wish to point out to you that the whole CPS movement will be endangered if the Estacada camp is adopted and administered by CPS.
>
> The purpose for which the camp is being set up is, at this time, purely a war one, the building of a logging road to obtain lumber for war purposes. When CPS accepts and administers a camp dedicated to what is at best a "1A-O" project, the line between "4-E" and "1A-O" has been obliterated. Here, it seems to me, not merely the individual but CPS as a whole has to take a stand as to what work is acceptable and what is not.
>
> It is argued that to accept the Estacada camp and to let the volunteers go there would be but granting them the same freedom of conscience which has been granted to all men who are in CPS. I doubt that there is any man here who is conscientiously impelled to go to the new camp. Rather, the man who goes is doing so because he likes to work with road machinery or because of the good food and comfort promised him. I am asking him to give up these things in order not to destroy the recognition given the position of those who are conscientiously opposed to such work.
>
> If CPS accepts this project, I can see it accepting projects closer and closer to outright war participation, until CPS becomes nothing more than "1A-O" without the uniform. I urge you to prevent our going step by step where we would never have gone in one leap.

Copies were sent to Mark Schrock, Harold Row and Dan West, an important Church of the Brethren peace activist. Gunterman's letter states and rejects the position of Mark Schrock and many of the men that the Three Lynx Camp should be staffed by men who did not feel that the project violated their consciences. This is essentially Bill Finley's argument in his article in the *Columbian*. Schrock took an expansive, pastoral view of conscience and recognized a variety of positions in the camp and men who were willing to participate. At this date it is impossible to know whether Gunterman's statement that men would go because of the food and comforts or the opportunity to operate heavy equipment is accurate, but it is true that life at Cascade Locks was quite spartan. Gunterman is making the "slippery slope" argument. If we accept this project that seems war related, but a bit distantly, what comes next? As he points out, men who were willing to serve the military as non-combatants had the opportunity to ask for and receive the 1A-O classification, as Lew Ayres and others in CPS had done. Gunterman and others felt that a sharp boundary between civilian alternative service and non-combatant military work needed to be maintained.

Gunterman also wrote to Mark Schrock restating the major points he had made to Paul Comly French, but adding that the amount of money ($250,000) and the fact that heavy road building machinery was being made available was clear evidence that the Three Lynx project was war related. He expressed his dismay that Schrock and the camp administration had not consulted the men before agreeing to the project. Schrock's careful response lays out the various positions on the matter and then concludes that he feels uncomfortable making decisions of conscience for everyone given the diversity of positions in the camp. Gunterman, a 1934 Reed College graduate, was one of the older and better-educated men at Cascade Locks. He was also part of the "left wing" there. In his diary he describes himself as "a Socialist and an atheist (Correction: I would never accept the term "atheist" as descriptive of me.)" He was also bitterly opposed to conscription. Reflecting on his attendance at a regional CPS conference in Berkeley in November 1942, he says:

> *The most important issue in our situation is, of course, conscription. But we who are in CPS camps may as well be honest about it: we are taking a stand against war in act, but against conscription only in words, and our words are only a feather floating in the wind. Having, then, let the issue of conscription go by, where then shall we take our stand? The*

point next in importance, it seems to me, is the question of the type of work we do.[59]

Gunterman represents the position taken by the CPS men whose opposition to war was more politically-based and exhibited the "resister" tendency. Others, whose views reflected the "servant" tendency, held the classic non-resistant position of the Mennonites and Brethren, which was that they should do what the government asked unless it violated individual conscience.[60] As in the Yamada incident, these two positions were in conflict. Gunterman and those who agreed with him wanted to force a confrontation with CPS, the Selective Service and the Forest Service. Others preferred to minimize the controversy by making Three Lynx project service voluntary.

A confrontation eventually arrived, initiated by Frank Rypcynski's request to Mark Schrock on November 9 to assign forty men, willing or not, to the Three Lynx project. Based on Schrock's response and Gunterman's observations in his diary, many fewer than forty men would have been willing to go. Even more important, Schrock's own position seems to have changed. His memo to Rypczynski, dated November 9, is very strong. Joe Gunterman, who at that time was skeptical of Mark Schrock's leadership, wrote in his diary, "It was a very good letter, and an amazingly good one for Mark."[61] Schrock's letter reads in part,

> *During recent months there has been an apparent trend in the direction of selecting and carrying out projects in the work program of our camp which have definite material military value. The men of our camp have, of course, raised varying degrees of objection. The objections, as I see them, are not because the tasks they were called on to perform were in themselves destructive. Rather because the obvious purpose of the project could not fail to identify the men working on them with the military program of our country. This unwilling involvement extends to all in our administration who likewise are concerned only to work for brotherhood and to give our testimony against all military methods and attitudes.*
>
> *I believe the various civilian and governmental agencies cooperating in the Civilian Public Service program had understood that it was being outlined to give opportunity for constructive work to men who are judged by their draft boards to be conscientiously opposed to the military method of solving human problems.*

The question inevitably then raises itself: "Are we now in the midst of a process in which some of the cooperating agencies are knowingly and deliberately attempting to change the basis of our working relationship, or is the trend unconscious on the part of those planning the projects, possibly because they are not aware of the real concerns which have led the men in our camps to accept this as the expression of their opposition to war and their faith in the way of brotherhood and understanding?"

Schrock goes on to say that it would be impossible for him to provide the forty men requested, although he would try to find as many as possible. He ends by asking, "I should like at this time in connection with this to request the Forest Service through you, first, to attempt to provide projects of definite national value without involvement in the war program, and second, to clarify to us the understanding on which you are cooperating."[62]

Schrock also writes to Harold Row the same day, requesting that "the Brethren Service Committee should clear with the National Service Board and Selective Service so as to have a definite understanding that we refuse to have anything to do with any project bordering in any way on military purposes." He then adds:

I recognize that we have agreed to stand with each man wherever he draws the line in regard to such participation, but it seems to me that it is certainly just as urgent that it be known that the Brethren Service Committee shall likewise draw a line and stand by whatever the results may be. I believe such a position would not weaken our stand either with the government or with the men but rather would strengthen it.

Schrock had clearly been listening to the men and had come to understand, and accept at least in part, the position represented by Joe Gunterman.[63]

News of the controversy spread. Bill Cable, who had transferred from Cascade Locks to the unit working in the mental hospital at Fort Steilacoom, Washington, wrote to Mark Schrock on November 2 to express his concerns about several work projects that seemed overly war related, including the Three Lynx project. Cable had heard that Schrock, "a Church of the Brethren pacifist, has been glorifying timber cutting and the proper selection of trees to beautify the forests, not mentioning that the timber is to be used to build ships, etc. to help in the war effort." He went on to say, "That just didn't seem possible for you of all people, who has been a pacifist in thinking for many years—probably longer than most of us have lived, to be doing such a thing and I won't believe it until I hear it from you." The letter closed by asking whether the Brethren Service Committee was doing anything about such war-related projects.[64]

Schrock's lengthy and thoughtful response clarifies the factual situation and points out that the Three Lynx project had been planned long before the war began and that it would provide a supply of timber long after the war was over. In addition he informs Cable that he has written to the Forest Service and to Harold Row to express his concerns. Still the pastor, Schrock notes that canceling the project will "win the disfavor of those men in Three Lynx who are most enthusiastic about the work there. But I have long since learned that at least in a CPS camp, regardless of what one does, there will be somebody who will be likely to seriously object." He ends by asking Cable to "still believe in the integrity of all those involved," whichever side they were on."[65]

Frank Rypczyski continued to press. On November 12, he wrote to Mark Schrock requesting thirty men to report for the Three Lynx Project the following Monday: "In order to comply with the regulations set forth on B-8 and B-9 in CPS Handbook, I do hereby request that you select 30 men regardless of their objections and have them ready to be sent to Clackamas River by 8:00 AM, Monday, November 16." Schrock's response on November 13 left no doubt as to his position:

> As has been previously indicated, it is my understanding that the men in CPS camps may be assigned by the technical agency to whatever projects the latter outlines, subject of course to the director's approval except in cases of projects that have more or less bearing on the military efforts of our national defense program. In these cases it is my understanding that the conscience of the men will not be violated and that if it seems clear to the director that the men cannot conscientiously participate in a given project because it is recognized as having a definite bearing upon the defense program, the director has no obligation to attempt to persuade or compel the men against their convictions.[66]

As in the Yamada case Mark Schrock's moral courage, combined with the strong stand taken by the men at Cascade Locks, had a national effect. In mid November, representatives of the Forest Service, Selective Service, M. R. Zigler and Harold Row, representing the Brethren Service Committee, and Paul Comly French, representing the

NSBRO met in Washington. At this conference, Zigler, Row and French indicated that they would be willing to abandon CPS rather than force men to work on a project in violation of their conscience. The Forest Service agreed to drop the project and a telegram was sent to the office in Portland directing that COs were not to be asked to work on the Three Lynx Project. In addition, all future projects having a military purpose had to be submitted to the chief forester in Washington for approval. Joe Gunterman notes in his diary entry for November 20, it was "a great victory for us."[67]

The Brethren Service Committee went on record opposing military-related projects. Its formal statement of November 11, concludes, "The Brethren Service Committee refuses to sponsor defense and near-defense projects which force men to violate their consciences. It also discourages projects which depend primarily on made work for their sustenance. These conditions being met, however, the Committee expects each man in camp to render a full day's work within the limits of his ability."[68]

When Harold Row visited the camp in July, he said "We have always regarded CPS 21 as one of our most significant camps." The events of 1942 show that Row's judgment was correct. The arrival of Lew Ayres had brought national attention, and Ayres's efforts to transfer to the medical corps had opened new options for COs. In the Yamada protest Mark Schrock and the men of the camp showed enormous moral courage and highlighted what is now regarded as one of the most unjust actions ever taken by the U.S. government. In protesting the Three Lynx project, they forced Selective Service and the Brethren Service Committee to clarify their policies concerning the kinds of work that the men in CPS could be asked to perform. As 1942 drew to a close, the camp had much to be proud of, even if the men did not realize it at the time.

CHAPTER FIVE
1943: In for the Long Haul

The final issue of the *Columbian*, dated February 1943, reported that "at 3:00 A.M. on January 28, fire completely destroyed the Mark Schrock library." The night watchman did not discover the fire, which was probably caused by faulty wiring, until it was too late to save anything. The winter weather frustrated efforts to fight the fire. There were two feet of snow on level ground and drifts three or four feet deep in other places. Although the paths had been cleared, the snow made it difficult to maneuver around the building. Care had been taken to ensure that the water system and hydrants were free of snow and ice, but the water pressure was quite low. The fire hoses and a bucket brigade were ineffective. Approximately two thousand books were destroyed, along with original works of art by campers. The library had housed the newspaper office and the music room, so both the office equipment and sound system were destroyed. This building, which had been remodeled by Kemper Nomland and Alan McRae, was regarded by the men as "the most used and the most valuable building of the entire Cascade Locks camp."[1] The loss of the library

Mark Schrock Library destroyed by fire in January 1943. (*Davis-Kovac*)

Reading room in the CPS #21 library. (*LC Sheets 4:S4*)

collection was devastating. Some of the men had brought their favorite books to camp and because of limited space in the dorms had stored them in the library. Mark Schrock lost most of his personal collection, more than three hundred books. Mabel Schrock also lost some prized books: music, poetry, photography and fine art volumes.[2]

Within hours the men began to build a new educational unit that they called the "New Athens," using the building that had been the recreation hall. As reported in the *Columbian,* "The New Athens is not a mere building; it is an attitude toward learning. It presupposes a cooperative, energetic and determined desire on the part of all to build a better educational program out of whatever materials are at hand."[3] Within a few months, the new library had been renovated by the camp architects with indirect lighting and attractive bookshelves. By the fall of 1943 when Don Elton Smith arrived, the library was restocked with books and periodicals and had once again become a center of camp life. Spaces were found for the other activities that the library had housed. Part of Dorm #4 was walled off to provide a lounge and music listening room. A corner of that space was set aside for the cooperative store. The ping pong table was moved from the recreation building to the end of the dining hall.[4]

Despite the defiant spirit expressed by the writer of the article in the *Columbian* and the resilience shown by the camp in dealing with a disaster, the fire was an accurate symbol of what had happened to the men of CPS #21 since the previous issue of the *Columbian* had appeared in November. Harry Prochaska said it well in his article

"Why the Change?" "After living in camp for a year, after a year of changing personnel and repeated failures in establishing permanent camp programs, the glamor and the challenge of our living together is exhausted."[5] The boring and exhausting work projects, the miserable weather, and the lack of challenging mental and emotional stimulation had drained all the initial enthusiasm out of the campers. Many of the COs were idealists who wanted to be of service to their country and to humanity, but those desires were frustrated by Selective Service, which preferred to keep them out of sight, and by Congress, which felt that they were getting off easy compared to those in the military. Transfers to side camps or to other permanent camps meant that educational and cultural programs could not be sustained. For example, Al Hastings started a chorus, then transferred to Fort Steilacoom with fourteen others. Large numbers of men had been moved to new camps at Placerville, California, and Waldport, Oregon. Also, there was continual movement between the main camp at Wyeth and the various side camps. The pacifist community that many of the men had hoped for had turned out to be impossible to build and maintain.

In early 1943 it was hard to see an end to the war. The United States military was engaged in brutal combat in both the European and Pacific theaters. After Pearl Harbor, the Japanese had pressed their advantage, driving the United States out of the Philippines and occupying the Solomon Islands off the coast of Australia. In an attempt to reverse the momentum of the Japanese advance, American forces invaded Guadalcanal in the Solomon Islands, and the bloody battle on that island had been raging since August 1942. After unilaterally breaking the Molotov-Ribbentrop non-aggression treaty, the German army had launched Operation Barbarossa and attacked the Soviet Union in June 1941. By mid-November 1942 they were at the gates of Stalingrad. United States forces landed in North Africa in November 1942 and were fighting their way toward the eventual invasion of Italy. The entire country had mobilized for war. Much of the industrial capacity of the United States was engaged in producing the arms and other military equipment for the allies. Food and fuel were rationed, and the civilian population was being encouraged to buy war bonds to support the massive military build up. The COs, who were committed to peace, felt increasingly isolated. An anonymous poem found in the CPS #21 files in Elgin gives a sense of how at least one man felt about the CPS experience:

ISOLATION
Time staggers onward
With the pace of a snail.
While dejected hearts
Answer back with a wail.
It drives one to drink
And it tempts you to rape
But these be only temporary
Avenues of escape.
It shatters one's mind
Beyond comprehension;
It drives you insane
Such degeneration!!
"It's better than foxholes"
Quoting W. Harold Row
But he failed to mention
Just specifically how
Away in these mountains
From civilization
We are destined to suffer
This inhuman colonization.

A year of ups and downs for the men at Cascade Locks, 1943 brought both significant accomplishments, the launching of both a literary magazine and the School of Pacifist Living, and a devastating disappointment: the cancellation of a CPS overseas relief effort. Several men chose to "walk out" of camp to protest what they saw as the injustice of conscription and forced labor without pay, and were sentenced to prison terms of as much as three years. On the other hand, assignees took on new leadership and administrative responsibilities in the camp.

Administrative Training Schools

As assignees began to assume administrative roles in the various CPS units, NSBRO and the three churches organized a series of special administrative training schools. The first occurred in November 1942; three more were held in February, May, and October 1943. Five men from CPS #21—George Brown, Dick Mills, Richard Anderson, Bob Case and Charlie Davis—attended these schools, which included a week in Elgin becoming acquainted with the work of Brethren CPS administration and three weeks in Washington, DC, organized by NSBRO.[6] George Brown and Dick Mills attended the first school, which began in Elgin on November 2, 1942 and then moved to Washington, DC. Bob Case, Richard Anderson and Charlie Davis were scheduled to attend the school that began on January 31, 1943, but at the last minute, Selective Service decided not to give Davis permission to travel, so he could not attend. Shortly before Davis was to leave the West Coast, Harold Row received the following telegram: "Selective Service refuses to pay transportation Charlie Davis to Washington. Connected with Yamada protest," and wrote to Mark Schrock on February 2, 1943 to provide further explanation.[7]

At that time, Davis was the assistant director in charge of the detached service unit at Fort Steilacoom where he and the other men in that unit had developed a relationship with Dr. Fred Ring and his wife Mabel, pacifists living in Seattle who had offered hospitality and assistance to the COs. Their daughter, Eleanor, a student at the University of Washington, wrote to Davis on January 16 asking whether one of the men would be interested in being her escort for a "girl asks boy" dance on January 29. Davis agreed to go, but on January 23 he wrote to Eleanor indicating that he was due in Elgin for the administrator's school on January 31 and would be unable to attend. He did provide a substitute, Loyd Schaad.[8] This exchange of letters was the beginning of a relationship between Davis and Eleanor Ring that led to their marriage in November 1944, a marriage that lasted until Davis's death in 2002.

Davis was cleared to attend the third training school and traveled to Elgin in early May for the first week of training at Brethren headquarters. He arrived in Washington, DC on Sunday morning, May 16, 1943, along with Lloyd Hall, a CPS #21 man who had transferred to Fort Steilacoom, and two other men from the West Coast. They had ridden the overnight train from Chicago. They spent the day "pounding the pavement, and completely exhausting our selves, but seeing most of the famed sights."[9] The next day the school began, when they heard presentations on the background of the peace groups that sponsored the CPS program: Mennonites, Brethren, Friends, Catholics, and War Resisters. The daily schedule was packed. Davis had a forty-five minute streetcar ride from the place he was staying to the Friends Meeting House on Florida Avenue where the sessions were held beginning at

9:00 A.M. each day. There were meetings until noon, an hour and a half for lunch, then sessions from 1:30 to 5:00 P.M. After a two-hour dinner break a final session ran from 7:00 to 10:00 P.M. Often the men used the meal breaks to ask specific, or more personal, questions.

The second day included discussion of differences in the administrative practices of the three church groups and a presentation by Paul Comly French about the work of the NSBRO. French emphasized the precarious position of CPS as the war casualty lists grew. The protests against CPS and the letters demanding that the 4-E classification be abolished came in regularly and usually in response to the effect the war was having on a particular community. For example, when the Iowa National Guard unit got hit hard, the letters came from Iowa. From the beginning, the agreement between NSBRO, representing the churches, and Selective Service was informal. From time to time, NSBRO asked Selective Service to clarify some policy. As Paul French told the men at the school, in such cases the resulting policy directive was generally "something very bad. That is, we have gotten Selective Service's maximum position from their legal viewpoint, which is a good deal different from actual practice." Writing to the Wyeth camp, Davis also provided a picture of NSBRO headquarters at 941 Massachusetts Avenue, a four-story brick building, now painted white, of 1890 vintage. The offices were small and crowded. Four people handled all the transfers in a tiny basement office. "The place is hot—there is lots of work of all kinds and I cannot envy the "lucky" boys here." [Many of them were assignees.] In my opinion, Cascade Locks is preferable to Washington—from the standpoint of convenience."[10]

On May 20, Colonel Kosch addressed the school primarily concerning the relationships between the technical agencies, such as the Forest Service, and the religious agencies to Selective Service. He was able to clarify a number of contentious issues related to discipline, the hospital units, and emergency farm work, as well as the working agreement with NSBRO. Kosch assured the men that discipline was the responsibility of the camp director, not the project supervisor. Apparently, the Forest Service supervisors at Cascade Locks had been doing a "good deal of miscellaneous disciplining" and consequently were "out on a limb." As Davis reported, "One of the most interesting sessions here" featured Paul French and Warren Mullin of NSBRO on the evening of May 20 "in which many matters relating to dealing with Washington" were discussed. One of the questions was pay for

CPS. The lack of compensation was a source of enormous discontent in the camps, and Mullin was "quite graphic in saying that it was an absolute impossibility, and an increasing one as the war goes on (if that is possible). He canvassed congress last year for some one who would introduce a pay bill for CPS, but not one man would risk his career by introducing a bill of the sort."[11]

Over the next few days the sessions covered "the problems of records, camp administration from the SSS [Selective Service] point of view (see various directives), health, reclassification, etc., mostly dealing with the legal point of view and the procedural technique for getting things worked through SSS, etc." On June 2, they "slugged out a 7 hour session on Camp Organization—government, etc.— education, recreation, etc."[12] Also, sessions on safety provided actual accident statistics. On June 18, after the school closed, Charlie Davis wrote to Paul French with a detailed four-page evaluation. His major criticism was that several of the presenters were poorly prepared and that several sessions would have been improved if the attendees had been given relevant information to review in advance. For example, the session on forms would have been much more valuable if the men had seen the forms previously. On the other hand, there was much that he found valuable, including the presentations by the Selective Service personnel. He made several suggestions for future schools including sessions on counseling and pacifist discipline: "Most of us have a very vague idea of pacifist discipline, and because of our lack of practical knowledge we have no real discipline. We should attempt to discover a pacifist blitzkrieg that would show results before men get out of our area of jurisdiction and into the hands of SSS." He ended by saying that "the weeks at the Administrator's School were by far more significant than any other comparable period in CPS. The whole program was valuable considerably beyond my expectations."[13]

Detached Service Committee

As opportunities for detached service in mental hospitals and training schools, agricultural units, and medical experiments became increasingly available, camp directors had to devote large amounts of time to the evaluation of the men who had applied for transfer and to writing recommendations. On January 5, 1943 Mark Schrock wrote to Harold Row to inform him that in an attempt to "secure more group participation and a greater sense of responsibility on the part of the assignees," a detached service committee had been formed at Cascade Locks. That committee, which was chosen by the camp council, would "function along with the staff in making the evaluations on BSC form #1, Supplement #2," the standard form for recommendations for transfer to special projects. Schrock assured Row that he would also take personal responsibility for the accuracy of the evaluations: "I shall, of course, recognize the responsibility of adding any additional information or any dissenting votes where it seems to me the case deserves a more complete or truer report." But it was clear that he had confidence in the men: "The men working on the assignment have been very cautious and careful in their evaluation, and I think fairly keen in their insight. They may, in fact, be more critical than the staff has been inclined to be."

Along with making the formal recommendations, the detached service committee was also "attempting to help each assignee think through his own relationship to the camp and the work, believing that some thought given to this by each assignee applying for special service may be helpful to him."[14] Forming the committee was a good idea. As reported in the *Columbian*, "Although it is too early to determine the advantages of this method of selection for detached service, the plan has been met with the decided approval of the camp."[15] Harold Row and the staff at Elgin found that the "evaluations accompanying BCS forms from your camp are about the most helpful that we receive. The most valuable feature is that the evaluation includes statements from both you [Schrock] and the members of the detached service committee."[16] As the number of opportunities for detached service increased, so did the work of the committee. In 1944, Jim Townsend commented that the evaluations "demanded much time of its members, often to the exclusion of many other vital pursuits."[17] The committee struggled to find both adequate and efficient methods of evaluation. Because of its importance, the detached service committee was one of the few committees that continued to function until the camp closed in 1946. Vic Langford, one of the camp leaders who served on the committee, regards it "as the most significant achievement at Cascade Locks."[18]

CPS #101

A major frustration for pacifists was the unwillingness of Selective Service, the Congress, and the administration to allow COs to do more meaningful work than was available in the CPS base camps.

A particular regret was their exclusion from overseas relief and reconstruction. In November 1942, after a year and a half of effort, Paul French finally received approval in principle to create a unit to train COs for reconstruction projects. Along with the useful work it would do, French was convinced that creating such a unit would help improve morale in CPS. On April 21, 1943, General Hershey created the Foreign Relief and Rehabilitation Unit, or Civilian Public Service Training Corps, also known as CPS #101. The men assigned to this unit were to pursue a twelve-month course of study in preparation for duty on foreign relief and rehabilitation. A central research and administration unit was established at the University of Pennsylvania that was to prepare data and curricula for the five units to be operated by the three churches. The Brethren program was to be held on the campus of Manchester College in North Manchester, Indiana, where the men would receive college credit.

The opening of CPS #101 provided an exciting opportunity. Eleven men from Cascade Locks (Henry Dasenbrock, Bob McLane, John Jahn, Ray Verbeck, Vic Langford, Al Orcutt, Russel Hoskings, James Albrecht, Julius Richert, Louis Neumann, and James Townsend) were accepted into the Brethren Unit. Charlie Davis was assigned to the central research and administration unit in Philadelphia where he would be the accountant and do some research.[19] As Henry Dasenbrock reports in his book, the Manchester program was headed by Andrew Cordier, a professor at Manchester College who later became executive assistant to the secretary general of the United Nations, with the rank of under secretary in charge of General Assembly and Related Affairs. After leaving the United Nations, Cordier was Dean of the School of International Studies at Columbia University and served as acting president of Columbia during the 1968-69 academic year. The courses were part of the regular college summer program, and contained regular students. The schedule was intense: eight to nine hours of class per day and a heavy reading schedule.[20] Seven major courses were offered during the two five-week sessions. Two of the courses discussed contemporary Europe and Asia; others dealt with social work and problems of relief and reconstruction. In addition, there was work on practical skills such as agriculture, home construction, public health and sanitation, and cooking and nutrition.[21]

CPS #101 was short lived. On June 30, 1943, just a month after arriving at Manchester, Henry Dasenbrock wrote home to report, "THE AXE

HAS FALLEN!!! The American Legion got hot about 'pampered' COs 'getting rewarded for un-Americanism' by getting 'college educations at government expense.' Pretty stupid misinformation but worthy of the Legion!"[22] The American Legion objections and articles in the press led to Congressional action that neither Kosch and Hershey nor Paul French and the NSBRO could overcome. Representative Joseph Starnes of Alabama attached a rider to a War Department appropriations bill on June 25, 1943 that prohibited using any appropriated funds to pay any military officers administering CPS. This rider would have effectively killed CPS. Paul French and Claude Shotts, an NSBRO staff member and a classmate of Starnes at the University of Alabama, visited the Congressman on June 26 to try to change his mind. Eventually, Starnes revealed his real objections and admitted that he "objected to having Mrs. Roosevelt mixing in the program" and visiting CPS camps. The Starnes rider was passed by the House, but did not survive the Conference Committee. Instead, the appropriations bill contained the following language:

> *That no appropriation contained in this Act shall be used for any expense pertaining to (1) the instruction, education, or training of class IV-E conscientious objectors in colleges, (2) the service of such conscientious objectors outside the United States, its territories and possessions, (3) the transportation of such conscientious objectors to or from any college or any service, or (4) the compensation of any military or civilian personnel performing any services with respect to the matters set forth in (1), (2) or (3) above.*[23]

Although CPS had been saved, all hopes for CO service in overseas relief and reconstruction were destroyed. As Harold Row wrote to the camp directors, "I hope you will use care in informing your camps of this action. It is possible that some benefits will arise from the action. However, it certainly will prove a very great disappointment to all of the men in CPS."[24]

The language of the bill did allow the Brethren Service Committee to continue to operate a reconstruction unit in Puerto Rico, which was then one of the most poverty-stricken areas in the world. Andrew Cordier went to Puerto Rico in the spring of 1942 to explore the possibility, and the Martin G. Brumbaugh Reconstruction Unit was created in June 1942. Service in Puerto Rico provided a meaningful outlet for CPS men who were interested in relief and reconstruction work. Four men from

CPS #21 (Dwight Hanawalt, William Coston, Alden Douglas, and George Mason) were among the original eleven traveling to Puerto Rico to begin the project. Dwight Hanawalt did not expect to be accepted into the program, because the rumor was that two hundred men from the then thirty CPS camps had applied. It appears that Mark Schrock wrote excellent recommendations for the CPS #21 men, because they were disproportionately represented among those chosen.[25] Other men from CPS #21, including Henry Dasenbrock, Harland Gibson and Paul Kindy, transferred to Puerto Rico as the effort expanded.

The Illiterati

Although the *Columbian* ceased publication in February, Bill Webb, Kermit Sheets and Harry Prochaska produced a new and different publication in the spring of 1943: a literary magazine called *The Illiterati.* As they wrote in the introduction, the magazine came about because each had "stoutly refused to cease pursuing his respective muse." Their interest was partly personal: "All writers, particularly budding ones, like to see themselves in print." But they also had larger aspirations: "The importance of art during these war times becomes emphasized as an attempt to see beyond the immediate blind focusing of the life and time of human beings to the aims of the state. This work has helped the men involved to see something beyond"[26] The first issue also included work by several men at the Waldport camp, including poems by William Everson, who later became an influential figure in the San Francisco renaissance, and by Glen Coffield, who published several small volumes of poetry during and after the war and ran the Grundtvig Folk School at Eagle Creek, Oregon, from 1947-1954. Hugh Merrick contributed a "musical caricature for bassoon solo," entitled "Ortmerz." Produced by mimeograph with a screen-printed cover, the thirty-six page magazine was designed and

Cover of the first issue of *The Illiterati* designed by Kemper Nomland. (*Davis-Kovac*)

Agnes, the "obscene" sketch from *The Illiterati* #1. (*Davis-Kovac*)

illustrated by Kemper Nomland. Copies of *The Illiterati* were mailed to interested persons around the country. Apparently someone in the post office looked at a copy and discovered Kemper Nomland's sexy little sketch of a nude woman, subsequently called Agnes ("the chaste, pure one"), and decided that the magazine was indecent. All the copies that had not yet been mailed were confiscated and destroyed. In response to an inquiry, the solicitor of the post office department stated that the issue had been declared unmailable because of the presence "of a figure of a nude female character."[27]

A second issue of *The Illiterati* was published at Wyeth in the summer of 1943. The introduction asks the question: "But is art important to pacifism?" and concludes that "It is as essential for the pacifist to present his philosophy to the haunters of libraries, concerts and galleries, as it is for him to include his philosophy in the relief and reconstruction he plans to carry on after the war."[28] This thirty-two-page issue, also designed by Kemper Nomland, was produced by mimeograph with a screen-printed cover, but also included two interior pages with colored screen prints. Two poems by William Stafford, a CO at the Belden, California camp, whose book, *Traveling Through the Dark*, won the National Book Award in 1963, were published in this issue. Stafford was named Consultant in Poetry to the Library of Congress in 1970, a position that is now known as poet laureate. Agnes again appears on page three, but in a smaller and less detailed version.

The major figure in *The Illiterati* was Kermit Sheets. When he was drafted in 1941, Sheets was a high school drama teacher near Fresno, California. As he explained in a 2005 interview, his pacifism came from his family:

So, in our family. . . [at mealtimes, before] asking in prayer for a blessing, my father would read a chapter from the Bible. And there was a phrase about the Bible, "Where the Bible speaks we speak; where the Bible is silent, we're silent." And I took that up as being true. And when the draft was coming along, I went to the Bible and two things just stood out for me – "Where the Bible speaks, we speak." So in this case the Bible spoke to me: "Love your enemies, be good to those who persecute you." Well how could I kill anybody and believe in the Bible? So that's when I became a conscientious objector.[29]

At Cascade Locks, Sheets mainly worked in the kitchen, washing dishes, cooking, and baking, and was the first chair of the education committee. He also worked as the librarian and served as cook at several side camps.

Sheets had enormous creative energy. He was an active member of the staff of the *Columbian*, beginning with the first issue. He contributed poems, short fiction, and art to *The Illiterati,* as well as serving as one of the editors. He also wrote two original plays that were produced at Cascade Locks. On October 19, 1942 Sheets, Harry Prochaska, Bill Webb and several other actors "inflicted *Stalingrad Statement* on the camp."[30]

Kermit Sheets reading on his bunk at CPS #21. (*LC Sheets 4:S26*)

Cover of the published version of
Stalingrad Stalemate. (Davis-Kovac)

Stalingrad Statement was a short play written by "krmtt zhiitzh" which he described as "a ukrainium in three acts." The play was performed in the chapel; Bill Webb had covered the walls with newspaper (classified sections) on which he painted a set: windows, doors, closets, kitchenware, and a wild Russian. The play was eventually published in mimeograph with a hand-painted cover that gives a good sense of the original set.[31] In a brief prologue to the published version written by Sir Pro Hack (Harry Prochaska), the play is described as an attempt to understand the siege of Stalingrad and the Russian resistance to the Nazi army. As Prochaska writes, "No one can understand Stalingrad and its significance in the ages to come unless he realizes certain aspects of the Russian temperament and how these aspects are being manifest in the history-making siege which today is claiming the attention of the world. The diversity of qualities in the Russian soul is seen in the persevering stand for the territory that was their fathers' for generations before."[32] The play, set in a one-room hovel outside Stalingrad, includes some classic Russian characters: a drunk, a musician, a dying consumptive, an idiot, a man and his pigeon (wife), and a Russian lieutenant.

The first act has no dialogue, just violin music and action: drinking, coughing, knitting, and belching. In a parody of Chekhov, the man who lives in the hovel owns a cherry orchard that contains the grave of his grandfather which he wants to preserve. The lieutenant wants the man to allow the enemy army to march through the orchard so they can defeat the Soviet army. He promises that the enemy will restore the old Russia. The dialogue includes all the themes of land, ancestry, and history that are essential to classic Russian literature. The play ends with the drunk shooting both the man and the lieutenant. Harry Prochaska played the pigeon, and his performance delighted Sheets: "I'm still laughing at Prochaska, the big repulsive Slav, who played the pigeon—he was sensational. Red food coloring smeared on his hands

Production photo for *Stalingrad Stalemate*. Man on the ladder is Harry Prochaska as the pigeon. Bill Webb, who designed the set, is in the bed at the rear of the photo. (*LC Sheets 5:3*)

and feet and face, gunny sacks swathed around him, a bandana over his head—he was a mess. With the stolid stupid, matter-of-factness, he slouched around the stage."[33] Bill Webb played the consumptive, coughing in the bed, but the other actors are unknown. Sheets was particularly pleased that the performance coincided with the meeting of the CPS #21 advisory board which at that time still included some Mennonites, whom he seemed to delight in outraging. In addition to *Stalingrad Stalemate*, Sheets wrote a parody, *The Mikado in CPS*, which was performed at Cascade Locks in February 1944 for a party attended by young women from Portland and Seattle. The scene was shifted from Tittipoo to Cascade Locks; the Mikado became the director of Selective Service, and Poobah, the Lord High Executioner, became the camp's assistant director.

Sheets's poem in the second issue of *The Illiterati*, "Katharsis at Wyeth," gives an insightful picture of camp life:[34]

> *A hectic meal*
> *frantically prepared*
> *scarcely tasted*
> *hastily cleared,*
> *notebook jammed into overcoat pocket*

out of camp
across highway
down rough road
over railroad tracks to the river

Down by the inlet
are three friends to be avoided
this no time for companionship,
joviality
and debate
are not sought here
but the nearness of quiet.

Scrambling up the rock
feeling the compulsion of being waited for
absorbing the zigzag of the rarely used trail
wind blowing wildly
up to the top
and five firs.

Back resting against the tallest,
hair flying
coat billowed open
the clouds change from pearl to amber
over grey swirls across the water.

Whom was I rushing to meet?

Frustrated by the mechanized arm of the state
by the church sold to the state
by expediency
by the habit of learned emotions
here
I seek release.

I meet no one
but the drop of the precipice
and the river below
— a fleeting temptation
ending in laughter
loud
wild

cock-eyed laughter
at the stupidity of man's self-seriousness

Cleansed
by a revived sense of the comic
I return
whistling a theme from Prokofiev.

Shortly after the war Sheets moved to San Francisco and became a founding member of an experimental theater, The Interplayers. Around 1950 he met the avant-garde film maker James Broughton and subsequently played the title role in Broughton's short film, *Looney Tom, The Happy Lover.* He also had a role in *The Pleasure Garden,* which won a special award at the Cannes film festival in 1954. At their home in San Francisco, Sheets and Broughton also founded the Centaur Press which published collections of poems by Broughton, Anaïs Nin, Robert Duncan, Glen Coffield, Madeline Gleason, and Muriel Rukeyser.[35]

The other major figure in *The Illiterati* was Kemper Nomland, an architect who had been trained at the University of Southern California. Nomland was also a talented artist and designer. After the war, he returned to Southern California to practice architecture. Initially, he worked with his father, where one of their projects was Case Study House #10. The founder of *Art and Architecture* magazine conceived of the Case Study House project as a way to create modern home designs

Kemper Nomland with his portrait of Kermit Sheets. (*LC Sheets 4:S13*)

for the post-war housing market in Southern California. Nomland became a sought-after architect. Another of his notable projects was the redesign of Moore Hall at UCLA. Along with his architectural practice, he continued to experiment with drawing, painting and ceramics.[36]

The School of Fine Arts at Waldport

When Morris Keeton, national director of education for Brethren CPS, asked for ideas for specialized schools, several men interested in the arts suggested a School of Fine Arts. William Everson at Waldport and Kermit Sheets and Kemper Nomland at Cascade Locks were leaders in developing a formal proposal for such a school. On October 5, 1943 Sheets wrote a letter to Morris Keeton, which outlined the proposal. "We feel that the group should be a producing group as well as a study group. This somewhat takes care of the question of who should come to the camp—those who have already well developed talents in some art form or those who are more or less beginners, desiring training. If the group is both producing and learning, then it can be for both experienced and beginning artists." The school was intended to be broad in scope: "All sorts of fine arts should be included: writing, music (composition and execution), painting, sculpture, creative crafts (ceramics, weaving, etc.), photography, play production." It was essential that it be a creative community: "You see, the danger we are attempting to avoid is the setting up of a typical academic curriculum—as one camper expressed it, 'organized classes with pedantic lectures and charts by ex-high school teachers.' That, at all costs, we wish to avoid."[37]

The proposal was approved by the Brethren Service Committee as long as an appropriate site could be found. On October 30, Morris Keeton wrote to Mark Schrock at Cascade Locks and Dick Mills at Waldport to let them know that he had asked William Everson and Kemper Nomland to "sound out their comrades-in-arts about the proposed school."[38] Initially, the thought was that the School would be located at Santa Barbara, but several circumstances made that site unsuitable, so instead the school was established at Waldport, Oregon, largely because a nucleus of those interested were already there. William Everson wrote a publicity brochure to be sent to all CPS camps inviting participation. That brochure, mailed on February 1, 1944, proposed a school of essentially the same character that Sheets had described. It also listed the facilities that included a printing press and type. In conclusion, Everson suggested that a fine arts group composed of pacifists should be different from most such communities, which were subject to "petty bickering, rivalries and scandals": "We believe, on the contrary, that the pacifist cause offers a unifying principle those communities do not possess; that the disruptive elements occasioned herein will not be greater than those evident in any active CPS unit. To all those who find themselves in agreement with the conceptions and the outline here presented we urge immediate application for transfer. The need is apparent; given the insight and the will, the returns can be memorable."[39] Kermit Sheets and Kemper Nomland both transferred to Waldport taking *The Illiterati* with them, and publishing two more issues. By issue #4, the magazine was printed on the Waldport letterpress with hand-set type. After the war, Kemper Nomland and William Eshelman, another member of the Fine Arts Group, took the press to Southern California where they produced two more issues, one in 1948 and the last in 1955.[40]

Writing, fine printing and publishing became major activities at Waldport where members of the Fine Arts Group founded the Untide Press.[41] The camp newspaper was called the *Tide*, so as a reaction, the Fine Arts Group called their newsletter the *Untide*. The Untide Press published several small poetry collections including *X War Elegies* and *The Waldport Poems* by William Everson, *The Horned Moon* by Glen Coffield, and *Generation of Journey*, by Jacob Sloan. In late 1945 the Untide Press published *An Astonished Eye Looks out of the Air* by Kenneth Patchen. Kemper Nomland's cover design for this volume was the inspiration for the design of the Pocket Poets series published by City Lights Books beginning in 1955.[42] Eventually, Martin Ponch transferred to Waldport and brought along another publication, *Compass* magazine. The last two issues of *Compass* were edited and published at Waldport. One of the printers at Waldport was Adrian Wilson, who later became internationally known as a printer, book designer and typographer and was a recipient of a MacArthur Fellowship.[43]

Writing and publishing were not the only activities at Waldport. There was an active theater group that produced several plays including *Tennessee Justice*, written and directed by Martin Ponch. This play was based on the court records of trial of nine African Americans and their pastor for draft evasion. To involve more members of the camp, regular play readings were also held. There were groups engaged in painting and also in handcrafts such as weaving and pottery. Music was another focus, both the study of music through listening to recordings and live performances. Among the musicians at Waldport was violinist Broadus Erle who eventually joined the music faculty at Yale.[44]

Canning and Book Discussions

During the summer of 1943, the need to prepare fruits and vegetables for canning consumed many evenings at CPS #21 and interfered with the educational program. Eventually, the camp found a creative solution and used the evening work as a focus for reading and discussion. A dozen or more men sat around a table, slicing peaches or stringing beans, taking turns reading a book out loud to one another. From time to time the reading was interrupted for discussion. In July and August, two books were read, *Humiliation with Honor* by Vera Brittain and *Brothers Under the Skin* by Carey McWilliams. If the work ran late, some of the time was used to listen to recorded music or a stimulating radio program with subsequent discussion.

The School of Pacifist Living

In addition to the School of Fine Arts, the Brethren CPS administration organized several other specialized schools at Brethren CPS camps to give the men an opportunity to study a particular field in depth. During the course of the war four other schools were developed: The School of Cooperative Living, which began at the Walhalla camp in Michigan and then moved to Wellston, Michigan when Walhalla closed; a School of Foods Management, held at three different camps; a School of Race Relations at Kane, Pennsylvania; and the School of Pacifist Living at Cascade Locks. Mark Schrock was interested in such a school and worked with Morris Keeton, W. Harold Row, and Dan West, the Brethren educator and organizer, to make it a reality. On August 2, 1943 Schrock wrote to Row reporting "very keen interest here among the fellows for such a school," and that the "Forest Service does seem strongly interested to have such plans for a school worked out for this coming winter." Finally, Schrock expressed his personal interest by saying that having such a school "would also make it seem to me more attractive for us to stay on as directors." He enclosed a copy of a letter from Bob Case to Dan West concerning the proposed school.[45]

The Brethren CPS office submitted a proposal to the American Friends Service Committee and the Mennonite Central Committee on August 12, 1943, for a school to be held cooperatively. The school would last for six months. Dan West was to be the director and spend the first six weeks and the last six weeks in residence. The original plans called for the school to open with between twenty and thirty participants, some of whom would be residents of Cascade Locks; men from other camps would be allowed to transfer with Selective Service approval. [46] The original target date for opening the school was September 20, but negotiation with the other church agencies, NSBRO, and Selective Service seem to have been slower than expected. Morris Keeton sent out a memo to all men in Brethren CPS on October 13 inviting them to apply for the school and setting the opening date as November 15. The school did open in mid-November with twenty-eight participants, including Mark and Mabel Schrock and Dan West. The members included some of the long-time members of the camp such as Les Abbenhouse, Richard Anderson, George Brown, Bob Case and Charlie Davis, and some very new arrivals including Don Elton Smith who had arrived just a few weeks before the school began. J. Henry Dasenbrock, who was then at a CPS camp in Virginia, transferred back to Cascade Locks just to participate in the school.[47] There were other transfers from camps around the country and enrollment eventually grew to about forty.

Dan West in the Columbia Gorge during his time at Cascade Locks. (*Brethren*)

Minutes from an early meeting on November 19, 1943, with twenty-one members and five visitors attending, show the group confronting some fundamental questions such as the meaning of the term "pacifist living," and even what they meant by "school." Was the school just to be for the members, or would they eventually write pamphlets or even a book? The ideas presented in the discussion were summarized in the minutes and various members volunteered to take those ideas and try to produce definitions of the key terms. Dan West encouraged them to put their most "profound thoughts in the vernacular" so that everyone would understand them and so that no one would feel inferior. They also agreed on a schedule for the following week.[48] After the first month of the school, Dan West wrote a memo summarizing where they were and setting out his objectives for the remainder of the time. He began by admitting that "This is a tough job" and that "we don't have the answers" but that they would need them to lead their lives. Because it was a tough and important task, one of his aims was "A sound job of work. No hooey. This is not a job for any kind of kidding." He also anticipated that there would be difficulties and disillusionment that the men would have to work through. The specific goals included:

1. *To help every person in the School develop into a steady, intelligent, creative worker for pacifist living; also to develop (slowly) a sound School morale. The members of the School should become "radiators."*
2. *To help develop new plans outlining the main "requirements" for pacifist living.*
3. *To help produce articles, letters, etc., to pass on our best.*
4. *To help write a book on pacifist living.*

West knew that these were ambitious goals, so they were rank ordered. The minimum was to achieve goal number one.[49]

The school was an ambitious undertaking. The men committed to eight hours of work per week in addition to the fifty-one hours of project work expected of them. They were divided into twelve study groups, each of which tackled a specific area related to pacifist living, by which they meant a total lifestyle not just conscientious objection to war. The twelve study areas were fairly well defined, but still broad.

1. *Pacifist Living in the Home*
2. *Pacifist Living Outside the Home in Face to Face Groups*
3. *Pacifist Living in Group Activities in the Community*

4. *Economic Implications of Pacifist Living*
5. *Pacifism and World Problems*
6. *Pacifist Living and Education*
7. *Pacifist Living, Non-resistance, "Second Mile," Non-violence*
8. *Philosophical Bases of Pacifism*
9. *Disciplines Necessary for Pacifist Living*
10. *Pacifist Lessons from History*
11. *Relation of Pacifism to Government and Functional Democracy*
12. *Pacifist Living and the Class Struggle*

Any one of these areas could occupy a lifetime of scholarship, let alone six months.

Dan West, the director, had been a member of the Church of the Brethren national staff for many years, primarily working in the area of youth education. West's style was informal and non-directive; he asked questions and led by example. He conceived of education as a process, not as an end. Unlike other visitors to Cascade Locks, West actually went out on work projects with the men. For West "dogged humility" was the best attitude for learning and planning.[50] A World War I conscientious objector, Dan West was an important, if unorthodox, Brethren peace activist. In 1932 he had founded "One Hundred Dunkers for Peace" composed of young people who were looking for the "moral equivalent of war." During the Spanish Civil War, West did relief work in Spain and after returning began what became known

Members of the School of Pacifist Living. (*Brethren*)

as the "Heifer Project," now called Heifer International, which sent milk cows to those who were hungry.[51] West's very sensible idea is that it is better to send a cow that can keep producing than powdered milk which will run out. He began talking about his idea shortly after returning from Spain in 1938, but the project really took shape in 1941 when some Brethren farmers in northern Indiana volunteered to raise calves for relief. The first heifers were shipped to Puerto Rico on July 14, 1944. Although West was uncomfortable with the compromise with the government that CPS represented, he did go to Cascade Locks. It is likely that West's personal relationship with Mark Schrock was one of the reasons that he agreed to lead the school. When the West family moved to a larger farm near Middlebury, Indiana, in 1950, one of their motivations was that the Schrock family farm was only a few miles away.[52]

The individual study groups met regularly, once or twice a week. Outside speakers were brought in to give talks and to engage in discussions with the entire school or with individual study groups. The men also took advantage of the Cascade Locks library, which contained about three thousand volumes at that time and had subscriptions to a large number of periodicals. Initially the enthusiasm for the project was high but seemed to wane as time passed. Henry Dasenbrock comments that in early 1944 the school continued, "but the first fine flush was gone and the intellectual activity at the end of a hard day had slowed." Dan West was no longer in residence, so the groups had to carry on alone. On February 14 Mark Schrock and his family departed for Indiana. Since Schrock had been a major motivating factor in bringing the school to Cascade Locks, his absence probably removed some of the enthusiasm. Still, many of the study groups produced long and thoughtful interim reports.[53]

The interim reports show the participants struggling with large and complex issues in a mixture of questions, information gained from research, primarily reading, and insights. An early interim report from Unit 2 entitled "Pacifist Means Used to Build a Machine for Violence," written by G. Bernhard Fedde, discusses ways that the pacifist perspective has allowed the military to rehabilitate disobedient soldiers and return them to duty and how the military used pacifist principles to deal successfully with occupied territories after World War I. It then concludes that if those means had been fully executed they would "abolish the machine they are helping," an important insight.

A later long report from the same unit includes, among other topics, a thoughtful analysis of pacifist efforts to influence governments, particularly the cases of Mohandas Gandhi in India and J. Ramsey MacDonald, the pacifist who served as prime minister of England in 1924 and again in 1929 through 1931. Although both Gandhi and MacDonald had some success, the report asks penetrating questions concerning how a pacifist can work in the political system, which requires compromise.

When he was drafted in 1943 G. Bernhard Fedde was a practicing attorney in Oregon. Born in Brooklyn, Fedde had received an A. B. in history from Williams College, attended Columbia Law School, and earned a J. D. from the University of Oregon in 1936. After he was discharged from CPS, he served as the chief relief administrator for the American Friends Service Committee in the British Zone of Germany in 1946-47 helping to feed half a million German school children. Fedde had spent a year at the University of Munich after graduating from Williams, so he was fluent in German. Because he was raised in a Scandinavian community in Brooklyn, he also spoke Danish, Norwegian and Swedish, language skills that served him well throughout his career, which included a year as legal counsel for the Lutheran World Federation in Palestine in 1949-50. Fedde settled in Portland in 1957 where he practiced law, including immigration, refugee and draft law, taught history and international law at Portland State University, and was active in Scandinavian heritage activities. He died in July 2007 at the age of ninety-eight.[54]

The report of Unit 6 on Education and Pacifist Living tries to develop a pacifist philosophy of education. Rather than promoting pacifism, which might turn into indoctrination, the report outlines a series of methods to educate children for "world citizenship." The more specific suggestions such as "read good books and stories not of heroes of war but of heroes of peace" and "teach a cooperative spirit instead of a competitive one, in play as well as in work" exemplify a pacifist perspective. The final section on world relationships includes the suggestion to "teach that military force in national hands is a grave danger to world peace, and that force of any kind must be used with restraint and wisdom," clearly a pacifist ideal. Although the writers of the report thought they were expressing a wider perspective, their core beliefs were evident.

Unit 10 took on a major challenge, to develop a pacifist philosophy of history. Their interim report makes a strong case for the importance of history: "If the function of the School of Pacifist Living is to create a new social order, we cannot unlock the future until we have the key to the understanding of the past." Their method was to study instances in which pacifism was tried, a small sample, as they admit. A number of case studies are proposed, but only one, an outline of British history from the Roman invasion through Henry VIII, is actually presented. If others were done, they have been lost. These interim reports are a tantalizing sample of what might have been accomplished had there been more time and resources. The agenda was ambitious, and the participants in the school had a unique perspective on the subjects they chose to study.

Dan West returned in March and summarized the accomplishments of the school. In a memo dated March 16, 1944 he repeated his view that the chief aim of the school was the "*development of exemplars* of the kind we want to see elsewhere—'radiators' of the spirit of pacifist living, and effective workers on that job." He pointed out the difficulty of developing community because "CPS men are generally soloists—they work and decide alone in the main; otherwise they would likely have gone with the current toward war." He then provided some suggestions for group living as a part of pacifist living. A participants' evaluation of the school was conducted in March after Dan West returned. West summarized the comments, positive and negative, of the participants in a one-page document dated March 30. The negative comments, or liabilities, centered on the enormity of the task, the lack of time, the lack of clear organization, and the diverse nature of the participants, which made it difficult to work together. The list of assets was shorter, but the members of the school thought that what they were doing was "appropriate to CPS" and that they had grown personally and intellectually. In a document dated March 31, West gave his personal evaluation. He recognized that he had overestimated "the work motive of a large part of the members." The school had several handicaps including the difficulty in obtaining outside speakers. Of the seventy-eight speakers invited, only thirteen came. Another problem was the lack of office help, so that some of the mechanical jobs, such as typing reports, had to be done by the students, which took valuable time. West did feel that the men had the intellectual capacity for the project, had identified the essential problems, and had begun to develop the techniques of thinking together needed for the task. Consistent with his philosophy of education, West commented on the growing senses of humility and "cooperativity" in the school.[55]

Don Elton Smith wrote in his unpublished memoir of CPS, "My hopes for the School were disappointed. I had dreamed we would find a great strategy for action or state some fundamental principles. Instead the School seemed to expire with only a whimper."[56] From a distance of sixty years, he suggested that there were several reasons the school did not accomplish more. One was transfers to side camps. Men were always moving in and out of side camps, disrupting the continuity. Another was Dan West's style of leadership, which was inspirational and hands off rather than directive.[57] Of course, the enormous size of the task made it almost certain that the results would not match the expectations. Entire books could easily be written about any of the twelve study areas, not something to be accomplished in six months by forty men working a few hours a week after long days in the woods.

Richard Anderson had a more positive opinion: "At least from my point of view, the purpose of the school—as the title says—was to help us figure out how to live the Pacifist life. The end result would be measured by how much we carried out the creed, not by how much we could write about it."[58] Dan West's strength as an educator was his ability to ask questions and to get people to think in a new way. From Anderson's perspective, West succeeded in doing this at Cascade Locks. West's first goal for the school was development of the individuals, but he did have three other goals which included the writing of articles and books on pacifist living. Unfortunately, these latter goals were probably more than could ever have been accomplished.

Walk Outs

Early in 1943 several men at Cascade Locks became disillusioned with CPS and "walked out" in defiance of the Selective Service Act. Mark Schrock described the situation in a letter to Lew Ayres on April 22, 1943:

> *CPS #21 has continued to boil. It keeps slopping over in the form of various men who have decided through the process that they could no longer continue on with the injustices of conscription. Probably you have learned that just at present Bill Webb and Nathan Barad are in the custody of the county jail at Portland and Charlie Hornig has gone*

AWOL and is back east, temporarily working in a hospital. Though I cannot help but believe that they must be mistaken as to the benefits of the step they have taken, nevertheless I must admire their courage and bravery in standing for the thing to the end which they feel to be right. I failed to mention that Philip Isely had also left camp after he had the assurance that the dissatisfaction of the Forest Service had convinced Selective Service that he should not be here. He, too, went east, worked with the War Resisters League until he was picked up by the FBI and is now out on bond. He will be returned to Portland for trial as soon as that can be arranged.[59]

Webb, Barad, and Isely were sentenced to three years in the federal penitentiary at McNeill Island, Washington, on May 10. Isely and Webb wrote and distributed detailed statements giving their reasons for leaving CPS.

Philip Isely had been, at best, a reluctant participant in CPS from the time he arrived. Charlie Davis described him as a "social alcoholic," someone dedicated to the way the world ought to be but not very practical about the way the world really is and not very tolerant of other people's views. He spent a lot of time lecturing men about the deficiencies of the CPS system.[60] Isely is a perfect example of the "resister" tendency. In August 1942 Isely's refusal to work was the subject of a staff meeting attended by Superintendent Frank Rypczynski and members of his staff, Mark Schrock and members of the camp staff, and Paul Comly French and Major Franklin McLean from the Camp Operations Division, both of whom were visiting Cascade Locks. The Forest Service supervisors had refused to let Isely work on the project because he had "slept on the job in utter defiance of all authority." Isely's position was that the government was "doing him an injustice."[61] This meeting seems not to have resolved the matter as Isely's walk-out statement clearly indicates:

Freedom of occupational choice is essential for the psychological welfare of man. It is also absolutely necessary for technological efficiency in any production system that is designed to serve human needs, by enabling each individual to exercise freedom of occupational choice that the decisions of the administrative authorities can be adequately checked and related to human needs. Otherwise the result is dictatorship — for the benefit of those in power.

It is because the Selective Service and Training Act of 1940 denies this essential freedom of occupational choice that I became constrained to refuse further compliance with it, and left CPS Camp 21 in February, 1943, and have remained away without permission as charged in the indictment.[62]

Bill Webb's position was both less extreme and more sophisticated. As he says in his statement, in the early days of CPS he "shared the vision with many other pacifists that in this program we would have opportunity to engage in a new and exciting experience in democratic and cooperative living." For several months he worked hard to realize that vision, including helping with the first issue of *The Illiterati*, but began to realize that something was wrong with the system. He had "expected the work program of the CPS camps to provide opportunities for real service to humanity" but found himself "doing work obviously less important than the work which I was doing before I came to camp." Like many other COs, he objected to the lack of pay for CPS men, but even further he criticized the agreement between the churches and the NSBRO and the government to administer the camps, which he characterized as a "serious compromise of principle" which "actually gained very little." He goes on to say that "the central error of the whole CPS program is that pacifists are administering the military conscription to one another."[63]

In April, 1943, Charles Hornig left camp, an act he announced in a letter to General Hershey. His reason, similar to Webb's, was that the work he was doing at Cascade Locks was not as useful to humanity as other work he could be doing. On February 2 he applied to Selective Service for reclassification so that he could accept employment in a hospital. He left camp to "indicate a need for reclassification. I hope your office and the local board can see fit to permit me to work for Humanity and my country without violation of my conscience or American democracy."[64]

In December, Alan McRae left CPS and issued what is best termed an absolutist statement:

This action is in part a means of clarifying my stand on the war issue. The ethics of warfare are the antitheses of those I hold to be essential to desirable relationships of men and nations. I do not voluntarily support any part of a war program. To accept even the conscientious objector provisions of this conscription involves participation in the military system. I can no longer do this and retain the integrity of my pacifist conviction.[65]

McRae also received a three-year sentence at McNeill Island.

In early 1944 Don Baker walked out, but received only a two-year sentence, indicating a change of attitude by the court. Bob McLane, who left in April, just a few months later, received a sentence of six months. In 1945, three men convicted of deserting from the CPS camp in Lapine, Oregon, were given four-month sentences in the same court. The federal judge in Portland thought that Selective Service was part of the military and he disapproved of its delegating its authority to a civilian camp director. Consequently, he felt that the assignees should be subject to military regulations. Giving light sentences was his way of signaling his disapproval. He hoped that the government would change its policy of prosecuting violations of the Selective Service Act in the Federal Courts. McLane wrote a four-page statement giving his reasons for leaving. He had considered walking out at the time that CPS #101 had been killed by Congress, but had been persuaded to stay. His statement indicates some of the reasons. As he says, "CPS, with all its many drawbacks, has been very profitable to me." He enjoyed some of the forest conservation work and built strong relationships with other COs. But, like McRae, he finally concluded that CPS was an unacceptable compromise with the government:

> *Hence CPS has been and is still what it appears not to be – a benevolent concentration camp administered by church agencies. This is the main trouble with CPS. We are not realistic enough to recognize that we are forced to stay here, are deprived of our rights (quote Colonel McLean) and allowed the opportunity of applying Selective Service regulations to ourselves, thinking all the while that we are operating the camps.*[66]

As the war progressed, more and more men left Cascade Locks and the other camps around the country. Sibley and Jacob report that in 1943-44, 3.4 per cent of COs prosecuted were walkouts; in 1944-45, the percentage had increased to 9 per cent.[67]

CHAPTER SIX

1944:
Transition to CO
Leadership of the Camp

The new year brought major changes to Cascade Locks. Director Mark Schrock resigned. After he and his family left for Indiana in February two assignees, Bob Case and Charlie Davis, were chosen as co-directors, leaving the camp entirely in the hands of the COs. In late summer a personnel committee was established, primarily to handle the sometimes contentious issue of assigning men to side camps. That committee functioned so well that it eventually became an executive committee for the camp, working with the directors to design and implement policy. Although the offering of formal classes had mostly been abandoned, a large number of outside speakers visited the camp and a variety of more informal educational efforts were undertaken. Near the end of the year the men began to compile a camp history.

The Departure of Mark Schrock

In November 1942, Mark Schrock wrote to Harold Row indicating that he would not continue as director of Cascade Locks beyond the summer of 1943. Mark and Mabel were interested in providing a more permanent and secure situation for their children, particularly in a rural and agricultural community. The Schrocks believed that their children "deserve and need a rural setting where they can have a part in observing and caring for growing animals and assuming responsibilities in a way that rural life alone permits."[1] In a letter to Lew Ayres in April 1943, Schrock clearly expressed his concerns about the effect that living at Cascade Locks was having on his children: "We wonder sometimes how long we should continue in our relationship to CPS, particularly because of the children. It does generate an abnormal environment for them."[2] Mark Schrock also felt a personal calling back to the rural life: "For a long time I have had rather a strong pull toward getting into a rural community and becoming indigenous to it, in the belief that successful local Christian units are the things out of which a peaceful and constructive world must be built."[3]

There is evidence that Schrock was getting tired of the pressures of the job. With two major incidents—the Yamada affair and the battle with the Forest Service over the Three Lynx project—1942 had certainly been a stressful year. Most of his personal library had been destroyed in the fire. Dealing with the wide variety of men, particularly those with strong political agendas, was wearing. As he wrote to Bill Cable in February 1942, "I have long since learned that at least in a CPS camp, regardless of what one does, there will be somebody who will be likely to seriously object."[4] Another concern was their living situation in the camp. The small director's house did not have a kitchen, so the family ate all their meals in the camp dining hall. The parents felt that private family meals were important for their children. One option that was explored briefly was to have them move to a house on one of the camp farms, about a mile and half away. That move was never made, but in the summer of 1943 the Forest Service added a kitchen to the director's residence, which was a significant improvement.

The Schrocks, however, were undecided about where they might settle. Their families were in Indiana, but they had been in the West for ten years and the "mountains, forests and canyons, and the greater freedom of action here may have spoilt us."[5] Over the next year Mark Schrock made several inquiries concerning possible positions. He wrote to family members and friends in Indiana about openings for pastors in the area. He contacted the Elkhart County Farm Bureau about the possibility of employment in the cooperative association, perhaps as the education director. He also corresponded with J. W. Lear, the executive secretary of the Pacific Coast region of the Church of the Brethren, about possible ministerial positions, or work as a regional coordinator. He also wrote to Dean Lowell Weiss at LaVerne College and to Andrew Cordier at Manchester College about setting up new programs at those institutions: work camps combined with academic courses, what we would now call service learning. He also inquired about the possibility of working with a project to assist in the resettlement of Japanese-Americans.

The improved living situation and circumstances at the camp, including the establishment of the School of Pacifist Living, kept Mark Schrock at Cascade Locks longer than he had originally intended. Eventually, the declining health of his father precipitated a rather sudden move to Indiana in February 1944. Some of the reasons can be found in a letter from Mark Schrock to his brother-in-law, Dr. Homer Burke:

I have gathered from mother that in addition to or a part of whatever physical difficulties were there, the senility is really the most disabling in its mental effects, though mother says she has little or no opportunity to discuss it all with the other members of the family. (I suppose more recently her much visiting among the children has given more opportunity, though she may have been reluctant to share.) Mother was suffering most deeply under the strain of seeing the developments in father while feeling completely unable herself to either help him or share with the other members of the family about it all. I have had a strong desire to be close enough to take a part of the load off of mother. It has seemed rather immaterial to me where we locate, though on the home farm might give the most easy and frequent contacts with both father and mother, I suppose. However, a smaller farm, with more time to give to other interests might have its advantages also.[6]

On February 13, 1944 the men of the camp hosted a farewell dinner for the Schrock family, complete with a printed program with the title "So long Schrocks." All the campers wore their Sunday best and the kitchen crew created a special dinner of roast chicken with apple dressing. There was a full program of entertainment. The camp musicians, Hugh Merrick, Leland Goodell, Don Chamberlin, Bob Carlson, Norman Haskell, and (Harold) Ike Bock all performed. There were readings and pantomimes and a farewell speech by Charlie Davis. A highlight was the "Overhead Quintet " of Charlie Davis, George Brown, Dick Anderson, Bob Case, Bob McLane and Bob Searles singing what Julian Schrock describes as "sort of the camp song," CPS Forever," which was sung to the tune of "Little Brown Jug." Julian remembers most of the new verse created for the evening

> *When I was free and on my own,*
> *My draft board called me on the phone*
> *They said to take a pair of socks,*
> *And take the train to Cascade Locks*
>
> *. . . (unknown)*
> *To spend the decade with the Schrocks*
> *But now they got out on parole*
> *And left us eight years in the hole.*
>
> *Ha, ha, ha, you and me*
> *CPS, how I love thee*

Ha, ha, ha, oh my yes.
How I love you, CPS.

The next day, their trailer packed, the Schrock family left for an eighty-acre farm near Bremen, Indiana, owned by Homer and Marguerite Burke.[7] Mark Schrock had been an innovative, patient, tireless and courageous director who was both loved and respected by the men in the camp. Joe Gunterman, who had been critical of Schrock in the Three Lynx incident, wrote, "My over-all memory of Mark Schrock is positive; in fact, he ends up as a minor hero in my years."[8] Richard Anderson, one of the first assignees, remembers the initial organization of the camp: "It was at this point that the unique qualities of Mark Schrock came into play. He immediately set out to create a climate where the focus was on each individual's capacities, dispositions, and energy."[9] Vic Langford, another camp leader, described Schrock as a "principled man, tolerant, [who] tried to satisfy a group of COs with *very* strong ideas of their own, some of which he must have found baffling."[10] Mark Schrock had facilitated the development of an unusual community. The future of the camp now lay with the men who would take over the leadership.

Selection of a New Director

When Mark Schrock announced that he was leaving Cascade Locks, the Brethren Service Committee was faced with the problem of finding a new director. Responding to the desires of the men for a more democratic selection process, a "conference method" was adopted. Essentially, the conference method meant that a selection committee, composed primarily of men from the camp, established criteria, collected information from candidates and references, and made a collective decision. The BSC had a representative on the committee, preferably the executive director, but the technical agency (for Cascade Locks, the Forest Service) did not. The guidelines for the conference method suggested that the process begin well in advance of the date the position was to be filled (at least six weeks) and that the members of the conference be carried on camp overhead so they could devote the required time and energy to this important decision. The conference method was first used to select the camp director at Cascade Locks. It then became standard practice for filling camp directorships in all BSC camps.[11]

The committee to select the new director of CPS #21 was composed of Bob McLane, Charlie Davis, Jim Townsend, Bob Searles, Bob Case, Bernard Fedde, Mark Schrock and Harold Row. It was a mature, well-educated group that included several camp leaders. McLane, Davis, and Case were all college graduates. Fedde was a lawyer. Townsend, one of the first to arrive at CPS #21, was a quiet scholarly man. Although Davis, Case and Searles were members of the camp administration, McLane was a sharp critic of CPS who walked out of camp shortly after the committee's work was completed. They developed a long list of qualifications, in no particular order:

1. *"Follow-thru" – the ability to convert ideas into accomplishments by himself and effectively thru others.*
2. *Christian spiritual motivation.*
3. *Should hold respect of the different groups in camp.*
4. *Should recognize the limitations of the administrative set-up and be willing to work within it. The attitude toward Selective Service, Brethren Service, and Forest Service should permit whole-hearted cooperation.*
5. *Ability to express and interpret well to groups in and out of camp.*
6. *Real and obvious concern for people.*
7. *Significant experience in CPS.*
8. *Ability to meet people on their own ground.*
9. *Ability and desire to identify himself with the campers.*
10. *Encourage camper initiative and participation in camp activities.*
11. *Understand group processes – growth, interaction, etc.*
12. *Concerned with understanding Selective Service – able to see their problems and good and bad points.*
13. *Youthful in spirit.*
14. *Good counselor.*

Twenty-three men were considered as possible candidates, including Grant McGuire, George Brown, Lee Lynne, Bob Bowers, Bernard Fedde, Charlie Davis, Bob Case, Dick Mills, Allan Barr, Art Casaday, Graham Hodges, Hank Dyer, Luther Harshbarger, and George Reeves.[12] Most of the candidates were not current assignees at Cascade Locks, but several of these men held administrative positions in the camp. George Brown and Bob Case were assistant directors. Dick Mills had been an assistant director and then became director of CPS #56 at Waldport. Charlie Davis was the camp business manager. The committee spent well over thirty hours in deliberations and selected Bob Case as director and

Charlie Davis as associate director. The committee felt that the director needed assistance at a higher level than that of an assistant director and that the two would complement each other. Although Davis held the formal title of associate director, the men considered the two to be co-directors.

The administrative duties were divided in the following way:[13]

Director (Case)	Associate Director (Davis)
Administrative relationships	*Camp management (kitchen, farm, laundry)*
Counseling	*Buying and Accounting*
Policies	*Records and Procedure*
Personnel committee	
Detached service committee	
Side camp meetings	
Coordination	
Personnel program	
Education program	
Religious Program	
Recreation Program	

The directors were assisted by four secretaries — personnel, religious life, recreation, and education — who were responsible for coordinating the program to which they were assigned. Two of the secretaries,

Charlie Davis as the "Okie Dope" in a CPS #21 skit. (*LC Blocher D41*)

personnel and education, were full-time, but the other two were half-time positions.

The division of responsibilities took advantage of the different strengths of Case and Davis. Case was an assistant director and had been a side camp director. Don Smith described him as having a "social worker" orientation, so he was well suited for the relational parts of the director's job. He had worked in the office with Mark Schrock and had been involved in a broad range of camp activities. Davis had a degree in accounting and was serving as camp business manager so he was already handling most of the responsibilities assigned to him. He had also served as the leader of the Fort Steilacoom detached service unit. Richard Anderson suggests that Davis's "most compelling trait was his pervasive wit; he could confront "tight spots" with witty remarks and could convert any "joke" into a "fable."[14] Both had attended an administrator's training school.

The co-directorship worked quite well and remained in place until Charlie Davis resigned in June 1945 to devote more time to his new wife who was living and working in Portland. Davis had married Eleanor Ring on November 22, 1944. He had written to Harold Row about his desire to be relieved of his duties as associate director as early as August 19, 1944. The job was time consuming: "During the past year I have not been able to do the work in a totally satisfactory manner even with spending considerably more than 51 hours per week on the job." Although he enjoyed the challenge, he had no time for other pursuits: "On the other hand, I have not read a book for more than a

Kenneth Keeton,
Assistant Director.
(*Davis-Kovac*)

year, my letters have all been official, my time for other camp activities has been very limited — and I don't want this type of thing to continue forever."[15] Davis once again became the business manager for the camp, and Kenneth Keeton, brother of BSC education director Morris Keeton, was selected as assistant director to handle the responsibilities that Davis had relinquished.[16] Case remained as director until he was discharged in December 1945. Don Elton Smith remembers them as able administrators: "Meals were prepared on time and were good, the farm ran quietly, overhead crews were selected without animosity. I don't remember any horrendously long and acrimonious general camp meetings."[17]

Charlie Davis went on to a long and distinguished career in business and civic affairs. Returning to Oregon in the early 1950s, after living for several years in California and Georgia, he worked for ElectroScientific Industries, a company founded by fellow CO Doug Strain, eventually becoming the chief financial officer. He served twice as public utilities commissioner in Oregon and as interim director of the Multnomah County Library. He was an active and influential member of the Portland City Club, an important civic organization, and was a pillar of the Oregon chapter of the American Civil Liberties Union, serving as board member and President for many years. When he received the E. B. MacNaughton award from the Oregon ACLU in 1973, the citation referred to him as the "conscience of his community." Partly because of his experience in the Yamada protest, he became a passionate advocate for Japanese-Americans. In 1999 he published a pair of articles in the *Oregon State Bar Bulletin* on Earle F. Bernard, the Portland attorney who defended Minoru Yasui, one of the Japanese-Americans who violated the curfew regulations of the Japanese relocation and incarceration in 1942.[18]

February Party and The Mikado in CPS

On several occasions, weekend parties were organized at Wyeth where young women from Portland or Seattle came to camp. The most memorable event was held on February 27, 1944, with "numerous members of the fair sex coming down from Seattle as well as several from Portland."[19] The men vacated and cleaned one dorm and one latrine for their use. The highlight, as noted in chapter five, was a Saturday evening production of *The Mikado in CPS*, written by Kermit Sheets. The campers played all the parts, male and female. "Bob

Group photo of a weekend party at CPS #21. (*LC Schrock 15*)

Searles as 'Yum Yum' made such a beautiful girl that he was afraid to walk back to the dorm without a bodyguard."[20] In Sheets' parody, the Mikado becomes the director of Selective Service, and Ko-Ko, the lord high executioner, is the acting assistant director of the camp. Nanki-poo, son of the director of Selective Service, is not a pacifist but is trying to hide from his father and from his father's choice for a wife, Katisha, by entering the CPS camp. The three little maids from school are "three little co-op girls." The play opens with the song:

> *If you want to know who we are*
> *We are the COs in CPS*
> *While the rest of the world's at war*
> *We the pacifist life profess*
> *We're in love with our fellow man,*
> *Whether yellow or black or tan —*
> *We'll save the world if we can. Oh. . . .*

As the plot unfolds, few aspects of CPS escape Sheets's delightful parody. Ko-Ko, the acting assistant director, is introduced by the chorus:

> *Behold our acting assistant director*
> *A pacifist of doubtful rank and title*
> *A dignified, though impotent officer*
> *Whose functions aren't particularly vital*

Ko-Ko responds by telling the story of how he obtained his position:

> *Taken out of CPS*
> *By a set of curious chances*
> *To director's training school*
> *Sent by BSC finances*
> *Wafted by a fav'ring gale*
> *As one sometimes in trances*
> *To a height that few can scale*
> *Save by long and weary dances*
> *Surely never had a male*
> *Under such like circumstances*
> *So adventurous a tale*
> *Which will rank with most romances.*

Ko-ko announces that the director of selective service is unhappy because not enough COs have been going 1-A-O, so he must draw up a little list of those who must become non-combatants in the military. That list contains many of the groups at Cascade Locks, each of which "never will be missed": the cheerful riser in the dorm who sings a merry note, the cook who makes the lunches you consume in the rain, the guy prolonging meetings, the dogmatic socialist, the gruesome culture vulture, the fussy vegetarian, the confirmed religionist, and those who have the plan to rescue all humankind. The song ends with the lines:

> *The task of filling up the blanks I'd rather leave to you*
> *But it really doesn't matter whom you put upon the list*
> *For they'd none of 'em be missed, they none of 'em be missed.*

The Gandhian influence on the pacifist movement is recognized when the chorus sings:

> *Satyagraha, satyagraha*
> *Gandhi, Tolstoi and Thoreau*
> *These our saints; and this our motto*
> *Violence must go — work for peace*
> *Work for peace for friend or foe.*

The Mikado, who is the director of Selective Service, arrives and reassures the men that he really is a civilian:

Though a major general, my rank's ephemeral
I'm civilian to the core.

In these two lines, Sheets expresses the CO critique that although the law says that the alternative service program is to be under civilian direction, it is largely run by the military officers in Selective Service. The Mikado goes on to state his real purpose or at least what many COs thought was his real purpose:

My object all sublime
I shall achieve in time
To make the punishment fit the crime
The punishment fit the crime
To see that each c. o.
Goes 1 A or 1 A O.
It's just my innocent merriment
My innocent merriment.

In the end, of course, all works out well. Nanki-poo marries Yum Yum and the play ends with the song:

The flowers that bloom in the spring, tra la,
Have nothing to do with the case;
We're stuck for the duration in CPS
We haven't the right to say no or yes;
We merrily sing to keep face,
Oh, we merrily sing to keep face.
And that's what we mean when we say or we sing
Oh bother the flowers that bloom in the spring![21]

As Don Smith commented, "Kermit certainly got *that* right: 'We merrily sing to keep face.'"[22]

The *Side Camp Newsletter* reported that "Following the play there was folk dancing until midnight, after which refreshments were served and social dancing took over until the wee hours."[23] On Sunday there was a panel discussion in the morning and a hike on the Wyeth trail in the afternoon.[24] Many of the women stayed over until Monday or Tuesday.

Fire Season

April brought the opening of fire season, which meant that the various side camps began to be populated. Often more than half of the nominal population of CPS #21, one hundred fifty to two hundred men, was assigned to side camps: Zig Zag, Timberline, Hemlock, Larch Mountain, Kingsley, and North Fork. Because of winter snows, two of the side camps, Timberline and Larch Mountain, were inaccessible until mid-summer, so the work of trail and phone line maintenance and other projects was carried out at lower-elevation camps, Kingsley and Zig Zag, until the roads were open. The Timberline camp was at six thousand feet on Mount Hood, near the spectacular Timberline Lodge which had been built by the WPA entirely by hand out of local materials in 1937. The Hemlock camp was across the river in Washington, where the men did general maintenance of the Wind River experimental nursery.[25]

The Departure of George Brown

In June 1944, the men of CPS #21 were surprised to learn that George Brown had requested induction into the army. Brown had entered the camp on March 5, 1942 and quickly become a leader. He was elected to the camp council a few weeks after arrival, and subsequently became education director. Brown attended the first Administrator's Training

Richard Anderson, Lawrence Morgan, Gilbert Grover and George Brown working in the CPS #21 office. (*Brethren*)

School in the fall of 1942. In the summer of 1943 he was chosen as assistant director, a position he held until February 1944 when the camp administration was reorganized following the departure of Mark Schrock and the selection of Bob Case and Charlie Davis as co-directors. Brown then went back to project work until his departure. One of his jobs was helping to regrout the walls at the Multnomah Falls lodge in the rain.[26] Never interested in physical labor, he had tried unsuccessfully to obtain administrative or research positions at other CPS camps or at Brethren headquarters.

A graduate of UCLA, Brown was a member of a periodicals group at CPS #21. This group met weekly, when each person presented a capsule of information from his favorite magazine. Brown's choice was *Business Week*. He was not a regular participant in sports or social activities but did enjoy a game of checkers.[27] Don Smith remembers him as bright, thoughtful and well read.[28] Others found him to be aloof and arrogant. Jim Townsend describes Brown's mind as "brilliant ellipses and strategic formulations with much consequent celebration to stimulate that ponderous equipment. It had apparently its own demands upon the outside environment to keep it in the status of lord and prince that it cried out to be."[29] Joe Gunterman might have seen Brown most clearly when he wrote, "Consciously or not, he plays a much more cagey game than I do. It is one of the things one learns in CPS, that even here it pays to play the cagey game."[30] What Gunterman called the cagey game is the practical road of compromise required in politics among other pursuits.

In a written statement to the men of the camp, Brown indicated that he had decided to join the army for "a number of personal reasons having little or nothing to do with my attitude toward war or my philosophy of social progress. Since the reasons are largely personal I do not care to go into them in detail. However, they [are] sufficiently strong to put considerable strain upon my mental and emotional equilibrium and have substantially interfered with the value of my contribution to the camp life and to the CPS program. I am taking this step as a method of releasing to some extent these strains." Brown was married, and his wife worked in Portland, routing trains on the night shift. Like most of the men in CPS he was under considerable financial strain. He had applied to NSBRO Dependency Council for financial help but his request had not been granted. He was also frustrated by his failure to obtain a more meaningful position in CPS. The report to

Brethren headquarters concerning Brown's request for reclassification indicates that he was under enormous psychological stress.[31] As he noted in his statement, joining the army decreased "the consistency of my thought and action in order to achieve more material gains, which seem necessary to me at this time."[32]

Financial exigency was a major reason for men leaving CPS to enter the military, either as non-combatants or as soldiers.[33] Between May 15, 1941 and May 31, 1944, 627 men had been discharged from CPS to enter the armed services. In the early days of the program, no distinction was made between those who entered as non-combatants (1-A-0) and those who entered as combatants (1-A), but subsequent records show that about one-third of the discharges were men who agreed to bear arms.[34] By March 1, 1945, the number had grown to 847, about seven per cent of the twelve thousand men who entered the CPS program during the war.[35] It is likely that Brown was looking ahead to a future political career. In a brief biographical sketch accompanying an article in the Spring 1946 issue of *Compass*, he wrote, "My attitude toward war is primarily intellectual revulsion at its stupidity, brutality, waste; I am acutely aware of inadequacy of existing social organizations and have deep desire to continue study of social organization putting knowledge to work in practical politics."[36] Brown was elected to Congress in 1962 and served eighteen terms representing the San Bernadino, California area. Throughout his career he was a strong supporter of science, serving as chair or ranking member of the House Science Committee. The National Academy of Sciences Research Library in Washington, DC is named in his honor. True to his pacifist perspective, he was a vocal opponent of the Vietnam War and voted against every defense spending bill during that era. He also fought for passage of the 1964 Civil Rights Act. Brown maintained his ties with the CO community and attended several of the Cascade Locks reunions organized by Charlie Davis. He died on July 17, 1999.

Personnel Committee

A persistent issue in the camp almost from the beginning was the selection of men for side-camps and for overhead positions. Some of these jobs, particularly overhead positions, were desirable, which meant selecting among several eager candidates. Others, such as assignment to small distant side-camps with poor facilities, were undesirable, so men accepted them grudgingly. In the early days of the camp, these decisions were primarily made by the staff. By mid 1943 Bob Searles had become the secretary to the Forest Service supervisor. Searles was well liked and perceived to be fair by the men in the camp, so he became the most important figure in the selection process. The supervisor could go to Searles, who would then find out who might be willing to go to a particular side-camp. Searles worked hard to organize a personnel committee that would be more representative of the men and would develop a system for selecting men for side-camps. This committee began to function in the summer of 1944, but its responsibilities and importance grew over the next six months.[37] The history and functions of the committee were eloquently described by Jim Townsend in early 1945:

> *Even more immediate in its bearing on the life of the camp is the personnel committee, that Gargantuan "many torsoed" body, which is at once deliberative, evaluative, legislative, administrative, judicial and executive. Beginning its career as a shipping agency to get men to side-camps, it has gradually become a functioning committee in most of the significant camp situations such as elections, reviewing of overhead responsibilities, setting up of priorities to determine how the burden of compulsion is to be shared though the whole camp group, and generating suggestions how sidecamp living may become more commodious and diversified. The decisions of the committee suggest a genuine emphasis upon educational, recreational and religious interests as against the bare compulsions of project work. In protecting these interests the committee has done little actual bargaining such as is customary in some of the other camps. Discussion with the Forest Service agency has not been deemed advisable as a practice. Consequently there have been only two or three such meetings. Reasons for not adopting such a custom are obvious from the attitude of the technical agency itself, which has not welcomed the idea of a "camper union." But the agency's distrust of delegation of the director's powers has not limited the committee's usefulness nor its place in camp life. The introspection of the committee has caused it to question its own usefulness, but also provided critical insight, method and procedure. The meetings have called for agenda and discussion disciplines. The spade-work with campers – with regard particularly to the priorities according to educational and other needs – has brought about an evolved knack of dealing with persons as persons. Although not the final instrument of all solutions, it has given the director considerable support in carrying out carefully matured decisions.[38]*

The personnel committee became a kind of executive committee for the camp, taking on the responsibility of removing men from overhead positions when their performance was unsatisfactory. Because the committee functioned so well, it was charged with the responsibility of selecting a new assistant director to replace Charlie Davis in the summer of 1945. When Bob Case was discharged in December 1945, the personnel committee again represented the camp in the selection of a new director.

A persistent problem at Cascade Locks and other CPS camps was the "evaporation" of committees as men were transferred or sent to side camps. This problem was solved with two innovations. First, twice as many men were selected for the committee as needed, with a priority voting system. If the nominal size of the committee was five, ten were elected and ranked according to the number of votes received. When a meeting was called, the five highest-ranking men currently in camp comprised the committee. Second, when it was time to elect a new committee a list of all men in camp was posted. Anyone who did not want to serve because he was uninterested or felt overworked could cross his name off the list. Once the list was reduced to those willing to serve, the priority election was held. This second innovation ensured that the men on the committee would take their work seriously.

Educational Efforts

One of the goals of Brethren CPS was to provide a vibrant and relevant educational program, a task made very difficult because of shifting schedules and frequent transfers to side camps. In the national office, Morris Keeton worked hard to find speakers who would visit CPS camps, often organizing tours on which a speaker traveled to several camps in the same geographical area. Throughout 1944, CPS #21 had an average of two outside speakers per month, many of them based in the Northwest. For example, two ministers from Seattle spoke at the Wyeth camp. Rev. Benjamin Davis, an African-American, gave two presentations on the race problem, and Rev. Fred Shorter, minister of the non-denominational Church of the People, talked about the relationship between the individual and society and the economic implications of Christianity. Some speakers, however, came from farther away. Dr. Alvin Brightbill, a professor of music at the Brethren Bethany Seminary in Chicago, talked about the problems of adjustment of soldiers returning from Italy. The educational report for July-August 1944, written by Jim Townsend, gave a glowing review:

*Professor Brightbill's racy and direct expressiveness gained him
the response from everyone. He seemed to have a wealth of personal
observations and anecdotes with which he pointedly reinforced his
thoughts on aspects of racism and postwar rehabilitation. The second
meeting was amplified by group singing. This time the discussion
centered about musical therapeutics with reference to war casualties,
and it flowed logically into comment on the place of music as an
art. The audience was enthusiastic. The third evening introduced a
more specialized topic, but succeeded well. We were shown the basic
distinction between sentimental and truly sincere church music. These
sessions were thoroughly enjoyed because they were well conducted and
the appeal was wide.*[39]

Sustained educational efforts within the camp were more difficult to
organize, but a book review group was initiated to stimulate reading
and to help men discover interests. A meeting was held every Saturday
night at which a person particularly interested in the book prepared
an introduction. This might be a lengthy period of selected reading
or a more informal overview. Some of the books presented included
H. E. Carr's *Conditions of Peace*, Robert Maynard Hutchins's *Higher
Learning in America*, and R. S. Lynd's *Knowledge for What*. One session
was devoted to the poetry of CO and CPS #21 assignee Glen Coffield
and a discussion of modern poetry. Several of the meetings had an
attendance of thirty. As Jim Townsend wrote, "The intention is to make
the programs of varied enough interest so that specific trends may be
discovered to help individuals who wish to pursue some particular
study."[40]

Aria da Capo

In late September Kermit Sheets wrote from Waldport to say that a
group of actors from the Fine Arts Group was ready to travel with a
production of *Aria da Capo*, an allegorical play with a pacifist theme
by Edna St. Vincent Millay. As James Townsend wrote to Don Baker,
who was serving his sentence at McNeill Island, "Why yes, it sounded
terribly exciting, so we tried to get a telegram off and all that last
minute stuff. One week later the players arrived and we stumbled
towards realization of the esthetic moment. But by then most of us who
were the planners were so tired with the exhilaration of planning that
we had little left to enjoy the spectacle with."[41] Townsend and Harry
Prochaska spent most of Saturday, October 7, preparing refreshments

for the occasion. The play was presented that evening. In Townsend's words it was:

> *a rather delicate, pastoral thing with a good allegorical theme: shepherds fighting over their lands and ways to feed their flocks (all symbolizing modern antagonisms between nations). It was acted fairly well, although some of the roles were simply mediocre. Manche (Langley) was the one superb actress. She dignified her role with the requisite amount of illusion, and appeared simply marvelously in her make-up and costume. Kermit (Sheets) was not up to his best. But he can be hardly blamed for that. The Friday night before the play, upon arrival in the morning hours, the players had a bacchanalian debauch, wherein they freely discarded emptied bottles and other conveyances until about four in the morning.*

Manche Langley was a Portland pacifist who had been a regular visitor to CPS #21. Shortly after Kermit Sheets transferred to the Fine Arts camp, Langley moved to Waldport, where she worked as a volunteer with the program. She accepted an invitation to come and help put on a play and decided to stay. She remained in Waldport

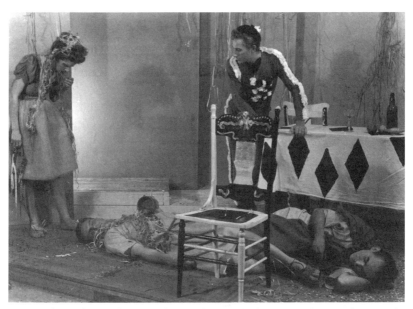

A scene from the production of Millay's *Aria da Capo*. Manche Langley, Enoch Crumpton, Kermit Sheets, and William Eshelman. (*LC Sheets 4:S70*)

for more than a year, eventually marrying Bob Harvey, a painter and writer who was a member of the Fine Arts Group.[42]

Attendance at the play was excellent; most of the camp was there and men came in from side camps for the event. Because expectations were very high, some of the audience were disappointed, partly because the acting was only fair and also because the allegory was not easily accessible to everyone. The following morning, there was a discussion with the arts group concerning the accomplishments at Waldport.[43]

Chain Gang Against Conscription

In his 1944 State of the Union message, President Roosevelt suggested to Congress that a national service law be passed. He continued to raise this idea. In an August 28, 1944 editorial *Time* reported that "Last week Franklin Roosevelt said he believed that the U.S. should give this idea (universal peacetime military service) some thought."[44] Roosevelt's arguments for the plan included military preparedness, but also included the importance of discipline and physical fitness.[45] Although *Time* supported the idea, Roosevelt's suggestion was controversial. On October 18, the *Christian Century* published a strong editorial opposing the passage of a conscription bill during wartime.[46]

A bill providing for permanent peacetime conscription for military training of all males between the ages of seventeen and twenty-one was introduced in the House (H.R. 3947) by Representative Andrew J. May of Kentucky, chair of the House Military Affairs Committee.[47] This proposal and other similar bills had the support of the Citizens Committee for Universal Military Training, the group that had headed the drive for the 1940 Burke-Wadsworth Act. Committee hearings were scheduled for November, so a group of men in CPS #21 mounted a campaign to oppose universal conscription; Jim Townsend called it the "Chain Gang Against Conscription," which started its work on October 21, planning and gathering reprints of essential articles. The socialists in Seattle contributed $50 to help cover expenses. The campaign involved both education and letter writing. As Jim Townsend wrote to Don Baker:

We've been overwhelmed lately with our work on an anti-peacetime conscription campaign. For two and a half weeks we've been going strong, and that means that about every spare moment of our time has been devoted to organizing and educating the camp as well as trying to

get something out for friends and trying to write important people and
organizations. In all a mammoth undertaking, which very few of the
other camps around the country seem willing to underwrite. Whether
from sloth or downright apathy, I don't know. We have bombarded
Waldport with letters asking them to buy a few postcards and send some
to Congress; but have heard no single word from them in reply. We also
have heard nothing from any of the other camps in this region.[48]

The members of the Chain Gang committed to write to one hundred people in their respective states urging them actively to oppose the conscription bills. By November 25 the campaign had begun to bring results. The Chain Gang received letters of support from around the country and the news from Congress was that there was considerable sentiment to postpone consideration of a universal conscription act until after the war was over.[49] Townsend wrote to Baker on November 29, "Somehow I'm not so pessimistic about the conscription bills as I was earlier. Evidently there has been enough protest from somewhere that the action had to be delayed on them until the next Congress. The Legion is very anxious to overcome the pacifist treachery and has issued a fine, patriotic statement calling for support."[50] Although the conscription bills were deferred in 1944, they were reintroduced in 1945, and extensive hearings were held in June.[51] After Roosevelt's death, President Truman called for the enactment of a universal military training act, and the Chain Gang was revived as the Committee to Oppose Universal Military Training in October 1945.[52] Letters, flyers, and posters were sent to key people, newspapers and friends all over the country urging them to oppose peacetime conscription.[53] Ultimately the movement for universal peacetime conscription failed, and no bill was enacted, a success in which the Wyeth Chain Gang played at least a small role.

History Project

In December 1943 L. S. Cressman, chairman of the Committee on Conservation of Cultural Resources for the State of Oregon, wrote to Mark Schrock inviting the camp to write a history of its development and accomplishments for the state archives, as part of a World War II history project.[54] After some delay, Bob Case and Charlie Davis asked Don Elton Smith to head up the project, and he organized ten units to write descriptions of the growth of administrative techniques, arts and educational efforts, the work project, CPS walkouts, and critical evaluation of the handling of COs during the war. Smith also invited the men to write autobiographies outlining their personal histories, the development of their thinking, their views of CPS, and their postwar plans. The project was quite successful. Smith was already in the process of writing a long paper on the "Development of Techniques of Administration in CPS #21," which became part of the history. Harry Prochaska wrote a history of the "Art Activities in CPS #21;" Smith and Kenneth Keeton prepared a study of the work project. Sanford Rothman and Max Ginsberg compiled a detailed "Analysis and Criticism of the Handling of Conscientious Objectors in World War II," to which Don Smith contributed a five-page addendum. Ten men wrote anonymous autobiographies ranging in length from four to twenty-four pages. The project took more than a year to complete, but in March 1946, Smith was able to send approximately two hundred double-spaced pages, comprising about forty thousand words of historical material that had been written.[55] In July 1946 when a list of historical materials that had been collected at the various camps and projects was compiled by the Pacifist Research Bureau, the CPS #21 materials were the most comprehensive of those on that list.[56] As James Townsend wrote in his educational report to BSC, "The whole history project has been of great promise, not only for the exercise of capabilities in discussing and writing, but also for the sense of becoming something that has given to the camp. Thus it has acted as a stimulus toward a more critical evaluation of achievement."[57]

Religious Life

After the departure of Mark Schrock, the camp's spiritual life received less attention, but in late November a religious interest group met to try to better attend to the needs of the men in the camp. A "religious cabinet" of twelve representing various points of view was formed to coordinate a program. Bernard Fedde was chosen as the interim secretary. Their first order of business was to organize a Christmas program that included decorations in the Dining Hall, Chapel, Office and Library, a special Christmas banquet, and both a Christmas eve candlelight service with readings and music from a choir and a Christmas day service with a guest speaker.

Fedde took the initiative to invite local ministers, primarily from Portland, to provide Sunday services. A diverse group of people were invited to provide sermons or to lead discussion groups. Because he was a Lutheran, Fedde had good connections with the Lutheran Ministerial Association in Portland, which did its best to provide ministers. For those like Fedde whose pacifism was derived from a strong Christian background, the religious program was essential. In a report to Elgin, Fedde provided more than a dozen suggestions of programs that might be organized to reach out to the cosmopolitan community of CPS #21. Mark Schrock had been both a capable administrator and a spiritual presence. Although Case and Davis were good administrators, some members of the camp deeply missed the Schrocks' pastoral presence.

CHAPTER SEVEN

1945-1946:
The End of the War
and the End of CPS #21

"Morale at the Wyeth camp clearly dropped during 1945."[1] Some of the men were entering their fourth year in CPS; most were entering their third. As detached service opportunities opened up in mental hospitals and medical and agricultural experiments, many of the men with the most talent and initiative had transferred to these more challenging units. Transfers to other camps and the constant shuttling of men back and forth to side camps made it difficult to sustain organized activities or even to plan ahead. Marriages suffered the financial strain of years without an income.

In February Charlie Davis presented an intriguing proposal, which apparently originated at the CPS camp in Belden, California. Because of the pressing need for prostheses for returning veterans, the Belden group had suggested that the camps begin making and fitting artificial limbs. Davis's idea was that the men at Wyeth would start making them in their spare time, taking orders from as many places as they could. Once production became efficient and a backlog of orders had built up, men would not be released to the Forest Service for project work, but instead would make prostheses, arguably work of more national importance than forestry. Selective Service would be in a bind. How could they prevent the COs from making artificial limbs for crippled soldiers? Even if the men were arrested and convicted for violating the Selective Service act, it was likely that a sympathetic judge would give them suspended sentences and send them back to camp to continue their valuable work. With characteristic enthusiasm, Davis began to research the details: canvassing opinions of the men in the camp, talking to lawyers, and investigating the costs of power tools. The plan never came to fruition, partly because Davis was unable to obtain the essential information, and partly because the war was winding down and planning for demobilization took precedence.[2]

Sessions on Psychiatry

Also in February 1945, J. Edwin Keller offered a series of talks on psychiatry. Keller, who had completed a year of graduate work in psychology at Northwestern, had transferred to Cascade Locks after twenty-one months of work on the violent ward of a mental hospital. He and his wife, Helen, who came with him, were also students of the general semanticist Alfred Korzybski, whose book *Science and Sanity* was quite well regarded at the time. The psychiatry study group was "in almost every respect a signal achievement." Keller had spent several weeks preparing for the sessions, which were attended by about thirty people. Keller's presentations were "put across with a degree of original insights that makes facts speak." Jim Townsend's descriptions of the sessions is lyrical:

> *He always builds discussion on previous experience rather than falling back on concepts as such. The structure of some of the talks has been almost like that of a musical fugue, with varied reference back to instances and experiences previously given. Through charts and use of gesture and a constant colloquial language the mind receives a several dimensional presentation, so vivid that it becomes, like folk-lore, a recurrent theme in camp. The barriers that so often separate class work from everyday life are not present, of course, which is an intrinsically valuable contribution itself.*[3]

Balloon Bombs

During April and May 1945, about fifty men were transferred to Cascade Locks from eastern camps to augment the fire-fighting crews, in response to the fear of forest fires caused by Japanese balloon bombs. Selective Service had suddenly ordered the transfer of 560 men to camps in Oregon and California. These mysterious moves had aroused the suspicions of Paul French who confronted Colonel Kosch. He would say only that the reasons were secret but that the men would eventually understand. When French independently learned that the transfers were due to the discovery of the balloon bombs, he was faced with a dilemma. On the one hand he did not want to reveal a military secret; on the other he did not think that he should make the decision for all the men in CPS, some of whom might object to participating in a military-related project. French also believed that Kosch had hidden the truth because he knew that NSBRO would object. Harold Row told French that NSBRO should defy Kosch and tell the men.[4] M. R. Zigler thought the best course was just to pretend ignorance, but French disagreed, arguing that they should not deceive the men. After considerable discussion, French went to see General Hershey, who was sympathetic. They worked out an unofficial agreement, which would allow the men to transfer out of the western camps after arriving and being told the reasons for their move. The churches, however, would be required to pay the costs of the second transfer.

Developed as a way to retaliate for the surprise bombing attack on Japan by Lieutenant Colonel James Doolittle on April 18, 1942, balloon bombs were probably the strangest secret weapon in World War II. Because the technological problems were so difficult, it required two and a half years to develop these instruments of terror: balloons that would travel over six thousand miles, drop their payload of bombs, and then destroy themselves. Beginning on November 3, 1944, the Japanese launched more than nine thousand balloons, of which three hundred were either found or observed in the United States and Canada. Experts have estimated that approximately one thousand balloons actually made it across the Pacific.

As early as the 1930s, Japanese meteorologists were aware of the high-altitude air currents now called "jet streams" and calculated they could drive a large balloon to North America in three days. The idea was simple. Launch a hydrogen-filled balloon to thirty thousand feet where it was caught by the jet stream. During the day, sunlight warmed the balloon, increasing the buoyancy, so it rose. The balloon was equipped with an altimeter, which was programmed to allow some of the hydrogen to escape when the balloon rose above thirty-eight thousand feet. At night, the balloon cooled and sank, so sandbags were carried as ballast. When the balloon descended to thirty thousand feet, the altimeter caused gunpowder charges to ignite, releasing two sandbags, one on each side for balance, and the balloon rose. The balloon went through a series of cycles during its trip across the Pacific. Once all the ballast was gone, the next gunpowder discharge released the bombs and lit a sixty-four-foot fuse which, after eighty-two minutes, ignited the hydrogen destroying the balloon and creating a bright flash of light in the sky. The Japanese research team concluded that a balloon with a diameter of ten meters was required to carry the required nine hundred kilograms of bombs and ballast.[5] The balloons were made of *washi*, a type of paper made from a mulberry that was much like American sumac. The sheets of paper were glued together with edible *konnyaku*, a flower paste from devil's tongue, a Japanese potato. Washi is tough and practically impermeable, an important property for containing the tiny hydrogen molecule that can easily diffuse through conventional balloon materials like rubberized silk.

The balloons began landing in California on November 5, 1944, and by November 6 were landing as far east as Wyoming. There were sightings or landings of balloons as far south as Nogales, Arizona, on the Mexican border, and as far east as Farmington, Michigan, ten miles from Detroit. On January 4, 1945, an incendiary bomb explosion was witnessed by two men working in a field near Medford, Oregon. The United States Office of Censorship immediately quashed the story and suppressed all subsequent publicity in fear that whoever was producing them might be encouraged to send more. Eventually, with the help of forensic geologists who analyzed the contents of the sandbags, it was determined that the balloons had come from Japan. The geologists were even able to discover which beaches in Japan had provided the sand. One of the bombs resulted in the deaths of six Americans. On May 7, 1945, about a month after the last balloons had been launched, Elsie Mitchell and five children were killed by a balloon bomb that exploded when one of the girls tried to pull the balloon from a tree. Reverend Archi Mitchell and his wife Elsie had taken some local children on an outing in the woods near Bly, Oregon. Reverend Mitchell was the only one who escaped, because he was a short distance away when the bomb was detonated. These six deaths are the only known casualties of World War II on the United States mainland.

Although the balloon attacks did not cause panic in the general population, the Army was deeply worried about the possibility of a large number of forest fires in the west. Along with the 560 COs who were transferred, three thousand Army troops were trained as fire fighters and stationed in the Northwest. After the various controversies at Cascade Locks over war-related projects, the Forest Service administrators were particularly concerned about CO attitudes toward fighting fires caused by the balloon attacks. Bob Case asked Don Smith to canvas the opinions of the men at Cascade Locks, but no one refused to participate.[6] Fortunately, the fires never came. The jet stream currents were favorable for transport to North America only in the winter, so the bombs landed on wet or frozen ground and did not cause any significant fires.

Hiroshima, Nagasaki and the End of the War

The destruction of Hiroshima and Nagasaki by atomic bombs on August 6 and 9 outraged the men at Cascade Locks. They immediately formed a steering committee for thought on atomic atrocity bombing and launched a vigorous campaign to send telegrams to national pacifist leaders. Most of the responses merely suggested writing letters to political leaders, but William Stafford asked, "How bad does it have to get before everyone objects? We feel that an opportunity exists now for forthright large-scale action." Bob McLane, writing from San Francisco after serving his prison term, was more realistic when he wrote, "Most of the people around here are of the opinion that the possible end of the war will very effectively reduce the effectiveness of any sort of graphic demonstrations."[7]

The bombings effectively ended the war except for the final peace terms. They also fed American arrogance. A CPS #21 newsletter quoted an editorial in the *Oregonian*: "We shall be glad to remember in years to come that we set an example of moral guidance, and a milestone for that civilization whose [unreadable word] was and is ours. By such a proof as this, the world observing, we have manifested our fitness to administer the secret of atomic energy." Jim Townsend, the author of the newsletter spoke well for the camp when he said, "Certainly arrogance has not perspective here," and quoted from *Measure for Measure* in response:

> But man, proud man,
> Dressed in a little brief authority,
> Most ignorant of what he's most assured
> His glassy essence, like an angry ape,
> Plays such fantastic tricks before high heaven
> As makes the angels weep.

Shakespeare is more applicable and contemporaneous than even the Oregonian and perhaps other voices of opinion because with him virtue is more than condescension.[8]

Relief Projects

In November 1945 Don Smith and Lyle Jones initiated an effort to send food packages to starving families in Europe. They drafted a letter to their fellow assignees at CPS #21 asking them to contribute twenty-five or even fifty cents from their monthly allowance to buy food for individual families in Europe. They obtained the names and addresses of those in desperate need from Dwight McDonald's magazine *Politics*. The average cost of a package, including shipping, was five dollars. The packages usually contained powdered milk, dried peas and beans, dried fruit and chocolate, but sometimes also razor blades and materials for shoe repair. Smith and Jones purchased the food, packed and addressed the boxes and filled out the customs forms. Initially they were able to send food to six families at a rate of two packages per week, but in February 1946 they had collected enough money to increase the rate to four per week. From November through March, they collected $201. The camp co-op store added $50 from the surplus when it liquidated its assets. At least forty-four packages were sent from the camp. Several men "took families with them" when they were discharged and continued to send food, and five assignees had sufficient funds to send packages on their own.

In addition, the men mounted a publicity campaign to raise awareness of the problem and to get people outside the camp to act. The first publicity leaflet was mimeographed, but soon funds were raised to print a pamphlet entitled "What's a Life Worth?" A committee chaired by Art Danforth wrote the text, and Bill Phillips provided the artwork. Ten thousand copies were printed and three thousand were stuffed, addressed and mailed by volunteers. The remainder were left with a committee in Portland.[9] For men who had spent the war working without pay, this was a remarkable act of generosity and commitment to principle.

Demobilization and Discharges

The first man discharged from Cascade Locks under the Selective Service "systematic release of conscientious objectors" program was Victor Scott, who left in late October 1945.[10] Demobilization of CPS was a public relations and political nightmare for Selective Service, which began planning for the end of the war in May 1945. The original plan, released on May 26, three weeks after the German surrender, involved a point system similar to that used for discharges from the military. CPS men would receive points based on length of service, age, and number of dependents. Those with the most points would be released first. The plan immediately came under attack from both sides. Advocates for COs complained that the provision that points be deducted for the number of days a CO had been AWOL or refused to work was too harsh. Others complained that releasing COs in the same proportions as soldiers would deprive society of the services of those COs who had valuable job skills. On the other hand, veterans groups such as the Veterans of Foreign Wars (VFW) and the American Legion thought that the plan treated COs too leniently, that CPS men would be released before those who had served in the military and perhaps take the desirable jobs first. Congress, which had never been sympathetic to COs, also responded negatively to the proposal. Representative Arthur Winstead of Mississippi introduced a bill designed to prevent using a point system to discharge men from CPS. The congressional action reflected the mood of the country, so General Hershey withdrew the plan. In September Colonel Kosch and Paul French met with three members of the House Military Affairs Committee including Representative Winstead, and they came to an agreement that Selective Service could begin the systematic release of COs from CPS camps in proportion to the numbers being released from the military. Although no formal point system was developed, releases were to be granted based on age, length of service, and numbers of dependents.[11]

At the same time that men began to be released, BSC was closing camps and detached service projects, so the population of CPS #21 increased. In October the hospital unit at Fort Steilacoom was closed, and several former Cascade Locks assignees, including Henry Blocher, Lloyd Hall, Al Hastings, Vic Langford, Sam Liskey, Bill Phillips and Loyd Schaad, returned. In preparation for its closing, the Waldport camp was reduced in size, and Kermit Sheets and Kemper Nomland returned to Wyeth along with other members of the Fine Arts Group, including the poet William Everson who had been the director of the Fine Arts School, William Eshelman, Broadus Erle, and Tom Polk Miller.

Nationally, more than 1,500 men were discharged from CPS in November and December 1945, including many camp leaders at Cascade Locks, some of whom had arrived with the first large group on December 5, 1941. Among those leaving at the end of 1945 were Director Bob Case, Business Manager Charlie Davis, long-time administrator Richard Anderson, and Librarian Jim Townsend, all of whom had been in CPS for four years. Charlie Davis and Sam Liskey were both discharged on December 21, 1945, a day when the Columbia

Gorge was iced over and the trains were not running. So eager were they to leave they decided to take a chance and drive to Portland along the two-lane highway that twists and turns along the gorge wall. As Charlie remembers, it was a harrowing trip, but with no other traffic they made it to Portland safely.[12]

Christmas 1945

In mid-December the weather turned very cold and brought hopes of snow for the holiday, but the temperature increased as the holiday approached. The men looked forward to four days off—two days of Forest Service holiday and the weekend. As Don Smith reports in his memoir

> . . . *a group of us in dorm 1 were discussing what we ought to do to prepare for Christmas. Before you knew it we were ripping out lockers, moving cots, fixing up lounge seats and cleaning generally. The boys cut a beautiful tree that we placed in the end of the dorm. We fixed fir boughs over the windows, around our lighting fixtures. Lyle (Jones) made a star for the tree top, put cotton on the branches. Bob Brown made a Yule log candle holder for our little table. We jumped in McCullough's car and drove to Hood River for a little shopping. (The roads were still icy and dangerous, but Mac is very steady.) We got cotton, candles, cheese, biscuits, and wine (loganberry, blackberry, sauterne).*
>
> *Upon our return, Lyle made a wreath for the door. Mac and Elbert Brubaker put some gorgeous pin-ups on the walls. . . . Went to dorm 4 at 8:30 for a little gathering Jim Townsend was having. Dave Orser and I went over, and then Carl Verduin came with a delicious loaf of date and nut cake he had just baked. We chatted and then read Thoreau's On Civil Disobedience . . . We said goodnite and good-bye to Jim who left early this morning for San Francisco.*[13]

Jim Townsend returned to San Francisco and enrolled at the University of California, Berkeley. He earned an A.B. (1948), M.A. (1951) and Ph.D. (1958), all in English. The subject of his doctoral dissertation was Chaucer's lyricism. He joined the English department at St. Mary's College in Moraga, California, in 1953 and served as chair from 1962 to 1973. He is listed in the college catalogs as "on leave" from 1975-1982 and as professor emeritus beginning in 1983. Townsend is remembered by his colleagues and students as a gracious, soft-spoken man with a slightly dramatic stutter, who was a excellent and devoted teacher

James Townsend in his study after the war. (LC Sheets 4:S38)

and a fine scholar. One former colleague, Brother William Beattie, who was academic vice president, said that "he had a wry sense of humor, which, on occasion, was quite stellar." Apparently, he enjoyed drinking scotch and tonic water, a combination that he discovered by accident.[14] Townsend died on December 4, 2002. St. Mary's College annually awards the Jim Townsend Scholarship in the amount of $7,000 to distinguished M.F.A. candidates in fiction and poetry. The award honors his profound service to students at the college and his lifelong dedication to the written word.

There were more parties and merrymaking through Christmas day, including a party on Christmas night at the Chamberlins, a CO couple who lived in one of the cabins near the camp, with cocktails, wine, and hors d'oeuvres. At least one man drank too much and was sick the next day. But all in all, it was a joyous time. The war was over, and men were being discharged in large numbers, returning home to resume their lives after two, three, or four years in CPS.

1946: The Last Months

The new year brought a new director to Cascade Locks, J. Wesley Smith, who transferred from Waldport, and a new assistant director, Howard Hamilton, but the camp was struggling. Although the camp would officially close on July 31, 1946, "it actually died sometime in December when morale, activities, and project work began to deteriorate."[15] The war was over, and because the COs were eager to go home and resume their lives their enthusiasm for project work disappeared. A significant number of the men in the camp were "resisters," actively opposed to CPS, and their attitude and actions overwhelmed the voices of those who supported the program. The long-time camp leaders who might have helped keep things together had been discharged. The hope of discharge resulted in a daily ritual described by Don Elton Smith:

> *Each day, promptly at 11:30, they appear in the office. Some sit, some stand, others mill around. A few talk in serious tones, some offer a few bits of shoptalk, others say nothing. In about twenty minutes, unless the mailman is off schedule, the sorted office mail arrives. Our subjects rise and peer intently as the envelopes are shuffled on the desk. "Nope, no discharges today," replies Hamilton to their inquiring looks. Slowly they retreat toward the door, wailing something like "If that thing doesn't come pretty quick I'll have to go back on project. I've only got three more days of furlough." There the drama ends, but only to be repeated the following day. To our perverse mind, it seems like a rather dreary, unemotional variety of the waiting room of a maternity ward. These men, of course, are awaiting a new birth of freedom.*[16]

Although the discharge notices may not have come as quickly as the men wanted, they did continue to come. During the first three months of 1946, more than two thousand men nationally were discharged, and another two thousand left in the next three months.[17] With the closing of the camp in sight, those who did not expect to be discharged soon took the opportunities to transfer to other sites, particularly detached service projects, as Don Smith did in March when he left for Elgin to do publicity and promotional work for the foreign relief program of the Church of the Brethren.[18]

The Seagull

There were some bright spots amid the gloom. One was the production of Chekhov's *The Seagull* in February. The play was directed by David Jackson and the set designed by Kermit Sheets. An attractive program was printed on the press that had been brought to Wyeth from Waldport. The cast included Kermit Sheets, who had returned from Waldport, and Tom Polk Miller, a Waldport transfer. Several wives of COs took part, including Louise (Goldie) Bock, and Hildegarde Erle, the wife of Broadus Erle, a violinist who had been a member of the Fine Arts Group.[19] Erle had been a professional violinist since the age of six. In 1948 he founded the New Music Quartet, the first quartet dedicated to performing contemporary music. After four

A scene from Chekhov's *The Seagull*. Louise (Goldie) Bock, Tom Polk Miller, Don Kirschner, Hildegarde Erle, Charles Ghent, Kermit Sheets, Eunice Picone, Robert Constable, John Land and Isabel Mount. (*LC Blocher Seagull 16*)

years as concertmaster of the Japan Philharmonic Orchestra in Tokyo, he joined the faculty of the Yale School of Music in 1960 and remained there until his death in 1977.[20]

The production team designed and built a set and acquired and installed the appropriate lighting. The six performances were documented in a series of photographs by Henry Blocher, who had returned to Cascade Locks from Fort Steilacoom, and by Bruce Dean.[21] The production was well received by those who attended.[22]

The CPS Strike and the Closing of the Camp

May brought a strike to CPS #21. On April 24 twenty-five men at the Glendora camp went on strike to protest the transfer of two men to the government camp at Minersville, California, which they portrayed as a "punishment camp." By May 15, the number had grown to eighty-two, and they were joined in sympathy by men at other camps including Wyeth. On May 13, the CPS #21 strike committee sent out a letter asking for funds to support their strike. In an undated press release clearly issued at that time, they stated that they were striking in sympathy with the men at Glendora, Minersville, and Big Flats, New York, who were protesting the continuation of injustice after the end of the war. The press release indicated that eleven men were on strike and that the number of men on the work project had dwindled to five. The strikers included several men who had been part of the Fine Arts Group at Waldport, including William Everson, Broadus Erle and William Eshelman. Lloyd Danzeisen prepared the press release and the letter asking for financial support. The men's fundamental complaint was that CPS was essentially slave labor because the men were not paid. Whatever justification there might have been for the camps during the war no longer held now that the hostilities had ended. Nationally, the strikes were mainly confined to a few camps, primarily government camps, and had little effect other than to make life at Cascade Locks more difficult.[23] Some of the men who had participated in the strike at Cascade Locks, Everson, Jehnzen, Crumpton, Erle, and Downs, had their discharges delayed by three months and were transferred to other camps when CPS #21 closed at the end of July 1946.

In the last months camp government, primarily the personnel committee and the educational program, completely broke down. As the population of the camp dwindled, enormous amounts of energy were expended in maintenance, just getting the laundry done and the wood stoves fed. Director Wes Smith and Assistant Director Howard Hamilton did their best to keep the camp going, but were faced with resistance from those who remained. One of their tasks was to prepare an inventory of all the property at the camp, a nine-page list ranging from supplies for the barbershop — electric clippers, shears and brush — to a panel truck. The inventory includes enough kitchen equipment to feed two hundred men, and one hundred rain suits that had been used by men working outdoors in one of the wettest places in Oregon.[24] The supplies and equipment were offered to Brethren projects first, and eventually for public sale. At the end of July 1946, the camp closed with the words of the last assistant director in his final report:

Well, the tents are finally folded, and with some regret and some satisfaction and with nostalgia for the experiences and fine friendships I had at CPS #21, I am
Very sincerely yours,
Howard D. Hamilton[25]

CHAPTER EIGHT

Conclusion

If Cascade Locks was "one of our most significant camps," the "Athens of CPS," how did this camp develop such a vibrant community that produced literature, art and music, a camp that could organize an effective protest of the removal of George Yamada and effect a change in national policy about war-related work, while other camps, such as Camp Simon, deteriorated into dysfunction? There are at least two reasons. One reason is leadership, especially the leadership of the first director, the Reverend Mark Schrock. Another is the characteristics of its assignees: as a large Brethren camp in Oregon that drew heavily on relatively well educated young men from California and the Northwest, Cascade Locks was able to develop a diverse educational and cultural program that could not be sustained in a smaller camp.

Leadership

Mark Schrock was a visionary director who showed a remarkable ability to work with COs from all backgrounds. Although one might expect a Church of the Brethren minister from a rural Indiana background to fit into the "servant" category, Schrock clearly exemplifies the "transformer" tendency in the Grimsrud typology. As he prepared for the opening of CPS #21, Schrock wrote a long letter to M. R. Zigler that lays out a vision for this new program. He conceived of CPS as a way to build a better society. He wrote:

> *The new opportunity combines several values:*
>
> 1. *We have the opportunity to discover and develop a new program and techniques of positive action for the protestor against evil. Of course, first of all, it will be a positive action program for protesting against war.*
> 2. *We have in this a new focus for Christian unity. Circumstances have brought together persons of all faiths and of no faith working together for a common objective which is felt by all to be worth more than life itself. It must be undertaken with full recognition of our differences, but without arguing about them . . . . This entire program should be a proving ground for our basic religious beliefs*

and fundamental assumptions, in a situation where we must test them by their fruits. All cooperating groups may well expect to find themselves growing stronger in the essentials of their way of life, while likewise increasing in their appreciation of the positions held by others. This will disturb those who have rested in smug complacency, and greatly exhilarate those who have hungered for truth.

3. *Our CPS camps should prove to be schools in Christian statesmanship, in which the fine arts of personal integrity and social reconstruction are combined and fostered. The cooperative living and integration of diverse interests in a democratic group will itself furnish the motivation and context for educational processes of unique and far-reaching influence.*

Schrock went on to discuss the kinds of people needed in the program. The first two characteristics are:

1. *Each person working in the program will need to be working vitally at his own life, keeping a growing edge on all frontiers. This is not the work for those who consider themselves full grown. Like the Kingdom of God, itself, this work must be entered like little children, else we can in no wise enter it.*

2. *Each person must give respectful consideration and treatment to all persons whether within the CPS group or outside. This must apply to those who are strangers to our code and to those who are violators of it. We claim the right of conscience and we must give the same right to others, without impugning motives.[1]*

This letter makes clear Schrock's administrative principles, as well as his own humility and humanity. Almost immediately, he set up a democratic camp government, which facilitated an extensive educational program. As Richard Anderson, one of the first men to arrive at Cascade Locks, wrote:

After the December 5 influx, the organizing task changed to one of integrating a group of human beings into a community. It was at this point that the unique qualities of Mark Schrock came into play, He immediately set out to create a climate where the focus was on each individual's capacities, dispositions, and energy. He conceived of a social and organizational structure that started with the individual camper. Decisions of critical relationships were not "handed down" from the

Director: they were formulated from the ideas of individuals — oftentimes in camp meetings. . . . So when the operation of the camp moved into high gear after December 5, Mark Schrock's idea that campers would determine community policies and practices energized a spirit of individual respect and freedom.[2]

Although the original government became unworkable and was replaced by what Don Smith termed a functional government, the principle of camp democracy was established. Another example of Schrock's commitment to democracy and community was the establishment of the Detached Service Committee in 1942 to involve the COs themselves in the process of evaluating men for transfer to special projects and, perhaps more important, his working with fellow campers in thinking through their goals and identifying their talents. The Detached Service Committee seems a Schrock innovation, not something he adopted from the practice of other camps.

Mark Schrock's continuing influence can be seen in the establishment of the Personnel Committee in 1944. Initially, just a committee to help assign men to side camps, this group became a kind of executive committee working with the director to formulate and implement policy. Bob Searles, who also fits into the "transformer" tendency, worked hard to establish this committee so that the side-camp assignment process would be more democratic, not just an administrative decision.

Mark Schrock was also a shrewd judge of talent. He quickly identified potential leaders and brought them into the administration of the camp: men such as George Brown, Bob Case, Dick Mills, Doug Strain and Charlie Davis. Both Mills and Case became directors of CPS camps, Mills at Waldport and Case at Cascade Locks. Although George Brown never obtained a higher-level administrative position within CPS, he had an extraordinarily successful political career. Strain went on to found and manage a successful electronics company, and Charlie Davis was a highly praised public utilities commissioner in Oregon. Shrock recognized their abilities, used them in appropriate roles at Cascade Locks, and when possible, promoted them for other positions in the CPS system. After Schrock's resignation, Bob Case and Charlie Davis became co-directors and proved to be capable administrators. The conference method established by BCS to choose new directors worked well in this case. Since Mark Schrock was both loved and respected by the men in the camp, his successors faced a major challenge, but they were equal to it and kept the camp running smoothly until the end of 1945, when both were discharged. Case's personnel skills and Davis's business acumen complemented each other nicely. Although the deliberations of the selection committee were not recorded, Mark Schrock was part of that group, and it is likely that his opinions were an important factor in the final decision.

In the two major confrontations that occurred in the summer of 1942, the order to discharge George Yamada and the attempt to set up the Three Lynx side camp, Mark Schrock showed enormous moral courage. In the Yamada case, he defied both Selective Service and the Brethren Service Committee, and put his job on the line. Although BSC ultimately supported him, it is clear from Harold Row's remarks that his challenge of the authority of Selective Service made the BSC leadership uncomfortable. Schrock also facilitated a community process in which the COs were able to discuss the matter thoroughly and make the decision to support his position. Other men in the camp, most notably Charlie Davis, were willing to take a public position opposing Yamada's removal, a decision for which Davis later suffered reprisals from Selective Service. In the hysteria that followed the attack on Pearl Harbor, the moral vision of Schrock and the men of CPS #21 was unusual.

Originally, Schrock's position on the Three Lynx camp was that those assignees who were willing to work on that project should be allowed to do so, but that no one should be compelled to work there against the dictates of his conscience. But over time, he came to understand and support the majority position that the project was too closely related to the war effort, and defied the Forest Service order to send a crew to the side camp. He also wrote a strong letter to BSC that resulted both in the formulation of a policy statement concerning war-related projects and in a national change in Forest Service policy. In taking this stand he had the support of a majority of the camp, which is another measure of the effectiveness of his leadership.

The actions taken by Mark Schrock and the men in the camp combined strong moral principle with sustained practical action, and were therefore quite effective. A similar balanced perspective was shown by the Chain Gang against Conscription in their effort to defeat the universal conscription bills in 1944 and 1945. Rather than make a symbolic but useless gesture, they worked systematically to influence Congress using the tools they had available, primarily letter writing. The men were also careful to inform themselves about the issues before acting. Their approach to political action was mature and sophisticated.

Schrock's commitment to "educational processes of unique and far-reaching influence" is exemplified by his work in establishing the School of Pacifist Living, which brought Dan West to Cascade Locks. Although the ambitious goals of that school were not fully achieved, its sustained effort to develop a program for peace could be implemented after the war. Several thoughtful reports were written, and the individuals who participated seemed to have benefited from the experience. The establishment of the Mark Schrock Library and its rapid rebuilding and restocking after the January 1943 fire, by men whose monthly allowance was $2.50, provide a further testament to the director's inspiration, and to the community's seriousness about education.

It may seem mundane, but Schrock's decision to rent the two farms to provide food was important to the continued success of the camp. Not only was the budget tight, there was wartime food rationing. The farms provided fresh produce, meat, eggs and milk, and the surplus was canned for the winter. The milk production was extensive enough that at one point Major McLean criticized the camp for serving too much. Schrock was also able to obtain fruit from local farmers and salmon from Indian tribes. As a result, the food at Cascade Locks was both plentiful and good, which certainly improved the morale of the camp. Because the men were engaged in hard physical labor an adequate diet was essential. Over the years, I have heard some stories from CPS alumni about too much zucchini, which resulted in zucchini ice cream, but no serious complaints about the quantity and quality of the food.

Characteristics of the Assignees

The Columbia Gorge is one of the most beautiful places in the United States. Although the weather can be miserable—rain, wind and ice—living in the gorge must have been an inspiration to many of the men. Charlie Davis regarded his time there as a privilege. Beyond the natural beauty, the location of CPS #21 as a large Brethren camp in the Northwest was an important factor in its success. Selective Service sent COs to the camp nearest their home but one that was at least one hundred miles away. This policy meant that most of the early assignees came from California, mainly the Los Angeles and San Francisco areas.

Although there were several Brethren communities along the Pacific coast, the population of CPS #21 also contained a large proportion of men from the mainline Protestant churches, such as Methodists, Disciples of Christ, and Presbyterians. At the close of May 1942, of the 185 assignees, the camp contained thirty-six Mennonites, twenty-two Brethren, twenty-three Methodists, six Presbyterians, six Friends, six Disciples of Christ, five Congregationalists, twenty-two men claiming no religious affiliation, and a scattering of members of other denominations. One hundred seventeen had come from California.

A major reason for the success of the camp was the number of assignees who were "transformers" in the Grimsrud typology, willing to accept the compromises of CPS and do their best to make a difference in the world. The large number of men who actively participated in the School of Pacifist Living is one example. The relief effort organized in 1945 by Don Smith and Lyle Jones is another. The various political actions and protests are also consistent with the "transformer" tendency. In his final letter to BSC, Howard Hamilton pointed out that the discharges in November and December 1945 of "men of the caliber of Charlie Davis, Bob Case, Rudy Potachnik, Lloyd Hall, Dick Anderson, James Townsend" crippled the camp. All of these men were "transformers." They were the men who made the camp work by taking on administrative positions, organizing educational efforts, and keeping the morale high. There were certainly a few "resisters" in the camp, Phillip Isely, for example, but the numbers seem to have been small, and until 1946 they did not have a significant effect on camp operation. There was also a small group of Jehovah's Witnesses, who were "separatists," but seemed not to have had a negative influence. Instead they just kept to themselves.

Whether it was the California influence or just luck, Cascade Locks had a large presence of writers, artists and musicians, some of whom became leaders in the artistic life of the camp. Kermit Sheets is the most prominent, but Harry Prochaska, Bill Webb and Kemper Nomland were also important in making the arts a central part of the community. Clearly Sheets's creativity and energy were essential to the establishment of the *Illiterati*, but he needed the others to make it a reality. He was also a key figure in the establishment of the Fine Arts Group at Waldport. His theater background led to the productions of *Stalingrad Stalemate* and *The Mikado in CPS*, original plays written in camp. Kemper Nomland's paintings and his work in design and illustration of the *Illiterati* are also noteworthy, as are the musical contributions of men such as Hugh Merrick, Harry Prochaska, Leland Goodell and Bert Olin. In the last year of the camp, the history project, organized by Don Smith, produced over two hundred pages of valuable material, more than any other camp of which I am aware.

Although it is difficult to make comparisons with other camps, the variety and quality of the educational efforts at Cascade Locks seem to have been unusual. Most camps had a variety of outside speakers, many of them recruited by Morris Keeton, the national education director, but the internally organized courses show remarkable talent and creativity. Even faced with the enormous challenges that transfers to side camps and detached service units presented, the campers continued to try new approaches The canning and book discussion sessions, and the Saturday evening book discussions, were creative ways to fit educational programs into the busy work schedule. From those informal activities came more formal courses such as the Keller lectures on psychiatry, which were an outstanding success. It is clear that learning and thinking were important activities in camp.

CPS #21: An Evaluation

Civilian Public Service represented an uneasy compromise between conscientious objectors and the government in the time of a popular war. The entire program was large and diverse, containing twelve thousand men in about 150 camps and detached service projects, so individual and camp experiences varied greatly. But Cascade Locks seems to have made the best of a difficult situation and created a community in which the individuals could prosper and grow intellectually, artistically and spiritually. From a distance of more than sixty years, the camp at Wyeth is an example of what CPS could achieve at its best.

The camp's intellectual and artistic environment facilitated a vigorous discussion of pacifism and its role in society. The School of Pacifist Living was the most organized and sustained effort, but as Don Smith remarked, the question of what it meant to be a pacifist was a continual topic of discussion at the regular bull sessions that pervaded camp life. The *Columbian* was filled with articles in which individuals expressed their individual perspectives on conscientious objection. One of the explicit goals of *The Illiterati* was to explore the relationship between art and pacifism. When men walked out, they often published statements that articulated their reasons for leaving. These statements were thoughtful reflections on the relationship between the individual and the state in a time of war and on the legality and morality of conscription. In 1945, as the war was coming to a close, the history project under the leadership of Don Smith provided an insightful assessment of the camp's history and collected ten autobiographical essays in which individuals told the story of what had brought them to camp and how their views had changed during their time in CPS.

Secondly, on several occasions the men of CPS #21 were able to engage in effective protest against what they regarded as injustices. The Yamada protest is the best example, but the Three Lynx protest might have been more effective because it resulted in a change in Forest Service policy and a strong statement from the Brethren Service Committee concerning war-related work projects. The Chain Gang against Conscription mounted a campaign to oppose congressional proposals for universal military training that ultimately were not enacted. It is hard to judge what effect the efforts of the men at Cascade Locks had, but they did organize a systematic effort to influence Congress.

Finally, although there were tensions along the way, CPS #21 functioned for four years as a democratic, cooperative community in which differences were respected and individual talents nurtured. Even in times of controversy, there is no evidence that the community split into competing factions. To be sure, there were divisions in the camp. The Jehovah's Witnesses kept to themselves; the "arts crowd" mainly bunked together in Dorm 4, where they played bridge and read the *New Yorker*. But as David Orser wrote:

My life has been changed in CPS. No one could live here for several years and not be changed somewhat. I have gained a greater appreciation and understanding of others. Nowhere before was I able to contact and observe individuals as here. I have learned that all people have their limits of courage and gratitude, yet interestingly enough on introspection, people possess a world of fascinating characteristics – some very similar to my own; others most different. Their lives, their very nature, have led me to think twice about the man I pass on the street; the face I see but an instant as I go by the door; the street car operator who smiles and gives me a nickel change, – not out of sentiment, you understand, but merely because each is a flashing figure from fiction.[3]

Don Smith summarized his CPS experience in the following way:

Every day in my CPS society I saw intelligent understanding of others, kindness and compassion manifested in one-to-one relationships. Immersed in such values/living skills, I learned to practice them, at least a little better.[4]

The poet William Stafford, who also spent the war in CPS, although not at Cascade Locks, talked about those who were "Saints of the Kingdom,"[5] by which he meant the CO community. These were men and women who were brought together by their willingness to stand up and witness for peace in a time when the rest of the country was solidly behind the war. When one talks to men who were in CPS #21, the deep connection they feel to each other is easy to sense. The common experience of the camp, the work, the bull sessions, the controversies, and the arts all had a strong effect.

Charlie Davis, who was not a conventionally religious person, often said when he got up from the dinner table that he was off to "do the Lord's work." That might mean paying the bills and balancing the checkbook, but more often it meant working on a political campaign or on a project for the ACLU or some other action to try to make the world a better place. In writing this book, I have come to understand that the men of CPS #21 were "doing the Lord's work" by showing the world that it was possible to take a stand for peace even in "the good war." As Michael Bess points out in his recent book, World War II was a morally complex event, but most important, an event that cannot be repeated.[6] The most important lesson of Hiroshima and Nagasaki is that another world war is likely to destroy civilization. Perhaps CPS #21, where a group of young men with nothing more to hold them together than the fact that they had said no to joining the military, were able to create a community where justice was a guiding principle, where the arts and learning flourished, and where individual differences were respected, can show us the way to peace. That is certainly what many of them thought they were doing, following the maxim of A. J. Muste: "There is no way to peace; peace is the way."[7]

Complete Roster of CPS #21

Name	Denomination	Drafted From
Abbenhouse, Lester C.	None	Seattle, WA
Abrecht, James W.	Baptist	Sacramento, CA
Alexander, Byron Eugene	Church of God of Abrahamic Faith	Hartford City, IN
Allen, Frank C.	Methodist	Portland, OR
Allen, L. Bernard	Methodist	Evanston, IL
Allstot, Richard E.	Brethren	Tonasket, WA
Anderson, Emil G.	Seventh Day Adventist	Enumclaw, WA
Anderson, Richard C.	None	Fresno, CA
Armentrout, John R.	Brethren	Cumberland, MD
Arroyo, Rene M.	Catholic	San Francisco, CA
Atkinson, William O.	Baptist	Los Angeles, CA
Ayres, Lewis F.	None	Hollywood, CA
Baima, Valentino D.	None	Grass Valley, CA
Baker, Donald E.	Methodist	Los Angeles, CA
Baldwin, Leo E.	Methodist	Fort Shaw, MT
Balster, Kenneth	Brethren	Santa Barbara, CA
Barad, Nathan N.	None	Los Angeles, CA
Barley, Delbert S.	Brethren	New Hampton, IA
Barnes, Charles A.	Methodist	Los Angeles, CA
Barr, Francis H.	Brethren	Nampa, ID
Barrett, Donal A.	None	Puyallup, WA
Barrett, John L.	None	Puyallup, WA
Bartleman, Francis B.	None	Los Angeles, CA
Bauman, Edwin F.	Old German Baptist Brethren	Modesto, CA
Baumann, Walter S.	Methodist	Glendale, CA
Beach, Kay H.	Methodist	Berkeley, CA
Beard, Paul William	Brethren	Westminster, MD
Bender, Charley	Advent Christian	Ferndale, WA
Benglen, Albert J.	Congregational Christian	Los Angeles, CA
Bentley, Harold G.	None	Seattle, WA
Berg, Glen E.	Evangelical	Spokane, WA
Berg, Orville C.	Pentecostal	Manteca, CA

Based on the Center on Conscience and War's *Directory of Civilian Public Service,* revised edition, 1996. List courtesy of J. E. McNeil of the Center.

Name	Denomination	Drafted From
Bergstrand, Robert W.	Mission Covenant	East Moline, IL
Berkey, Eldon E.	Jehovah's Witness	Kirkland, WA
Bese, Albert B.	Mennonite Brethren	Bakersfield, CA
Beyreis, Louis J.	Seventh Day Adventist	Bellflower, CA
Birdsell, Edward F.	None	Chicago, IL
Birky, Elden W.	Mennonite Old	Albany, OR
Bishop, Andrew J.	Brethren	Aumsville, OR
Bishop, Charles O.	Brethren	Aumsville, OR
Bishop, Montford H.	Mennonite General Conference	Lansdale, PA
Bjornum, Arthur O.	None	Seattle, WA
Bledsoe, Norman E.	Jehovah's Witness	Bremerton, WA
Blocher, Henry D.	Brethren	Pomona, CA
Block, Ervin F.	Evangelical Lutheran	Nicollet, MN
Boaz, Jacob Gladden	Brethren	San Diego, CA
Bock, George H.	Methodist	Nappanee, IN
Bock, Harold (Ike)	None	Nappanee, IN
Bohrer, Albert E.	Mennonite Central Conference	Normal, IL
Borntrager, Floyd J.	Mennonite	Bloomfield, MT
Borntrager, Mahlon H.	Mennonite	Bloomfield, MT
Bowman, Clarence E.	Brethren	Seattle, WA
Bowser, Max J.	Brethren	Fresno, CA
Boyd, Warren F.	Old German Baptist	Modesto, CA
Brandt, Lloyd Carleton	Brethren	LaVerne, CA
Brandt, Lowell D.	Brethren	Elgin, IL
Brechbiel, Kenneth O.	Brethren	Poplar, MT
Brooks, James E.	Christadelphian	Jourdanton, TX
Brooks, Wayne O.	Assembly of God	Marysville, WA
Brown, George E.	Methodist	Los Angeles, CA
Brown, H. Merle	Brethren	Mount Pleasant, PA
Brown, Herbert L.	Brethren	Ontario, CA
Brown, Jack G.	None	Los Angeles, CA
Brown, Milton L.	None	Compton, CA
Brown, Richard A.	Friend	Puyallup, WA
Brown, Robert E.	Methodist	Urbana, OH
Brown, Wayne E.	Methodist	Fort Wayne, IN
Bryant, Raymond W.	Brethren	Hoxie, KS
Buckner, John H.	Brethren	Pulaski, VA
Buelteman, Herbert O.	Methodist	Detroit, MI
Burkholder, Donald L.	Brethren	Octavia, NE
Burkholder, Joe D.	Mennonite	Nampa, ID
Burkholder, Winfield C.	First Century Gospel	Brooklyn, NY
Butler, Arthur D.	Brethren	Detroit, MI

Name	Denomination	Drafted From
Cable, William H.	Brethren	Syracuse, IN
Calkins, Glenn D.	None	Seattle, WA
Campbell, Victor L.	Pentecostal	Great Falls, MT
Canady, Noel J.	Christadelphian	Bee Branch, AR
Carlsen, Henry W.	None	Petaluma, CA
Carlsen, Wilmer	None	Los Angeles, CA
Carlson, Robert B.	Baptist	Riverside, CA
Carter, Robert P.	Brethren	Ashland, OH
Case, Claude W.	Brethren	Everett, WA
Case, Robert E.	Presbyterian	Oakland, CA
Catlett, Richard R.	Methodist	Springfield, MO
Cessna, Harold M.	Brethren	Kansas City, MO
Chamberlin, Donald B.	Presbyterian	Lebanon, OR
Chandler, James M.	Brethren	Kremlin, MT
Charlesworth, Ray C.	Disciples of Christ	Toledo, OR
Christenson, Gerald C.	Brethren	Seattle, WA
Cinco, Rudolph J.	Catholic	Euclid, OH
Claassen, Albert J.	Mennonite General Conference	Paso Robles, CA
Clardy, Charles G.	Church of Christ	Los Angeles, CA
Clawson, Larry D.	Baptist	Los Angeles, CA
Click, Maurice A.	Brethren	Bridgewater, VA
Click, Victor M.	Brethren	Bridgewater, VA
Cline, Jay W.	Brethren	Staunton, VA
Coffield, Glen S.	Methodist	Carthage, MO
Coffman, Barton E.	Jehovah's Witness	Yakima, WA
Cogburn, Travis J.	Church of Christ	De Leon, TX
Cole, Kenneth E.	Baptist	Santa Paula, CA
Coles, Charles E.	Moslem	Newark, NJ
Constable, Charles R.	Friend	Blanchester, OH
Cooley, Charles F.	Methodist	Warren, OH
Cornell, Boyd B.	None	Middleton, ID
Cornell, Douglas H.	Methodist	Leslie, MI
Coston, William P.	Methodist	Inglewood, CA
Cover, Chester D.	Brethren	Modesto, CA
Crain, Delbert E.	Brethren	East Akron, OH
Crawford, Hollie W.	Methodist	Stockton, CA
Crist, Dwain M.	Jehovah's Witness	San Marcos, CA
Crull, Bobby R.	Brethren	Wabash, IN
Crumpton, Enoch A.	Methodist	Chico, CA
Cutler, Maynard A.	None	Spokane, WA
Dahl, Carl B.	Mennonite Brethren	Reedley, CA
Danforth, Arthur L.	None	Snyder, NY
Danzeisen, Lloyd M.	Brethren	Brookville, OH
Darrow, Denton R.	Friend	Caldwell, ID

Name	Denomination	Drafted From
Dasenbrock, John Henry	Brethren	Ontario, OR
Davidson, Bertrum M.	Open Bible Standard	Terrebonne, OR
Davies, William J.	Presbyterian	Oakland, CA
Davis, Bircie L.	Church of God	Dutton, AL
Davis, Charles	Presbyterian	Anaheim, CA
de Bourbon, Prince Louis P.	None	Oklahoma City, OK
Deach, Charles A.	None	Parkdale, OR
Dean, Bruce Leroy	Disciple of Christ	Alhambra, CA
Decker, Boyd E.	Methodist	Cottage Grove, OR
DeCoursey, Wesley F.	Brethren	Nampa, ID
Dirks, Abe	Mennonite Church of God in Christ	Bonners Ferry, ID
Ditmars, Lloyd G.	Brethren	Washington, KS
Ditmars, Ray G.	Brethren	Washington, KS
Doramus, Richard S.	Brethren	Kuna, ID
Douglass, Alden C.	Presbyterian	San Francisco, CA
Downer, Daniel B.	Baptist	Los Angeles, CA
Downer, Prescott W.	Baptist	Los Angeles, CA
Downing, William	Jehovah's Witness	Everett, WA
Downs, Warren F.	Methodist	Salem, OR
DuBois, R. Eldon	Brethren	Rocky Ford, CO
Erle, Broadus J.	None	Sarasota, FL
Eaton. John B.	Church of Christ	Corbett, OR
Eck, David	Mennonite Church of God in Christ	Winton, CA
Ehrman, LeRoy M.	Jehovah's Witness	Fort Wayne, IN
Elmore, Floyd B.	Jehovah's Witness	Tulare, CA
Elmore, Roscoe D.	Jehovah's Witness	Tulare, CA
Eshelman, William R.	Disciples of Christ	Pico, CA
Etter, Harold W.	Brethren	Brookville, OH
Everson, William O.	None	Berkeley, CA
Fairman, Wirt H.	Methodist	Girard, OH
Fast, Walter	Mennonite Brethren	Glasgow, MT
Fedde, G. Bernhard	Lutheran	Eugene, OR
Fee, Gerald	None	Oakland, CA
Fillmore, Donald William	Brethren	Biggs, CA
Finley, Ernest Willard	Brethren	Oroville, WA
Fletcher, Ray	Brethren	Ventura, CA
Flora, Glenn W.	Old German Baptist	Brookville, OH
Follis, Paul E.	Brethren	LaVerne, CA
Force, Daniel N.	Congregational Christian	Los Angeles, CA
Forrester, Walter F.	Lemurian Fellowship	Inglewood, CA
Forsyth, Brian	Essene	Elismore, CA
(known at CPS #21 as Hugh Merrick)		

Name	Denomination	Drafted From
Foucault, Allan L.	Friend	Seattle, WA
Fox, Roy D.	Free Methodist	Modesto, CA
Franz, Arthur J.	Mennonite General Conference	Salem, OR
Frentrup, Benjamin	Church of Christ	San Antonio, TX
Friesen, Willmer J.	Mennonite General Conference	American Falls, ID
Fry, Amos E.	Mennonite Old	Willamina, OR
Gahler, Lester E.	Mennonite	Canby, OR
Gallaghan, James H.	Episcopal	Oakland, CA
Gandy, A. Elwood	Brethren	St. Cloud, MN
Garber, Emory L.	Brethren	Crown Landing, CA
Garber, Maynard	Brethren	Staunton, VA
Garber, William F.	Methodist	Compton, CA
Gaubatz, Edward G.	Pentecostal	Oakland, CA
Gensinger, Leonard D.	Brethren	South Bend, IN
George, Clarence W.	Methodist	South Laguna, CA
George, Keith H.	Friend	Seattle, WA
Gerig, Ernest	None	Salem, OR
German, Franklin W.	Presbyterian	Bellingham, WA
Getsinger, Boyd L.	Latter Day Saints	Lorenzo, ID
Ghent, Charles	Christadelphian	Portland, OR
Gibson, Harland	None	Arbon, ID
Giesbrecht, Pete	Mennonite Church of God in Christ	Winton, CA
Gillin, Chalmer C.	Brethren	Mineral Point, PA
Ginsburg, Max H.	Jewish	Brooklyn, NY
Good, Bernard E.	Methodist	Whittier, CA
Goodell, Leland A.	Methodist	Portland, OR
Goodrich, Earl R.	Congregational Christian	Medford, OR
Graham, James R.	Friend	Madison, WI
Gregory, Wayne T.	Brethren	Olympia, WA
Grover, Gilbert N.	Old German Baptist Brethren	Modesto, CA
Guengerich, Charles E.	Brethren	Altadena, CA
Gullander, Karl A.	Congregational	Oakland, CA
Gunterman, Joseph F.	None	Sacramento, CA
Haag, Walter E.	Brethren	Whittier/Los Angeles, CA
Haggen, Clarence M.	Congregational	Seattle, WA
Hall, Lloyd A.	None	Payette, ID
Hamilton, Howard D.	Disciples of Christ	Greenfield, IN
Hamilton, Ormond	None	Seattle, WA
Hamm, Eldon R.	Brethren	Centerville, MI

Name	Denomination	Drafted From
Hanawalt, Dwight L.	Brethren	LaVerne, CA
Harmon, Wendell E.	Brethren in Christ	Upland, CA
Harris, H. Vance	Brethren	Fernald, IA
Harris, William F.	Friend	Cottage Grove, OR
Harrison, Lloyd R.	Christadelphian	Elgin, TX
Hartzler, Clarence	Mennonite Old	Portland, OR
Harvey, Melvin M.	Brethren	Waterford, CA
Haselden, Clyde L.	Baptist	Minneapolis, MN
Hasenbank, Raymond Paul	Evangelical & Reformed	Alma, KS
Haskell, Norman	Disciples of Christ	Santa Ana, CA
Hastings Allen B.	Methodist	Phillipsburg, KS
Hausske, Harland A.	Congregational Christian	Portland, OR
Heald, Hiel E.	Friend	Newburg, OR
Heisler, Gareth W.	Brethren	Etna Green, IN
Helriegel, Robert W.	Episcopal	New York, NY
Henderson, William F.	Congregational Christian	Long Beach, CA
Herbert, Robert W.	Methodist	Oak Park, IL
Higbee, Charles E.	Methodist	Los Angeles, CA
Highman, Walter A.	Christadelphian	Detroit, MI
Hildie, Wilfred R.	Lutheran	Seattle, WA
Hillen, Lawrence R.	Lutheran	Leigh, NE
Hirst, Jesse A.	Christadelphian	Huntington Park, CA
Hoffman, Emerson L.	Brethren	Berlin, PA
Hoffman, Vernon S.	Brethren	Muscatine, IA
Hogrefe, Ralph E.	Jehovah's Witness	Creswell, OR
Hoke, Cassel J.	Brethren	Nappanee, IN
Holcomb, Lee B.	Jehovah's Witness	Newport, WA
Holderreed, Elzie R.	Brethren	Oakville, WA
Holland, Walter R.	Triumph Church of the New Age	Philadelphia, PA
Holmes, Hillard M.	Disciples of Christ	Puente, CA
Holt, Melvin	Disciples of Christ	Rickreall, OR
Holtzman, Paul D.	None	Beverly Hills, CA
Hopson, Frank E.	Jehovah's Witness	Los Angeles, CA
Hornig, Charles D.	None	Los Angeles, CA
Horst, Adam	Assembly of God	Glendive, MT
Hoskings, Russell	Methodist	Redlands, CA
Houger, Beryl W.	Nazarene	Spokane, WA
Howrey, Harold C.	Church of God	Gresham, OR
Hudson, Edgar E.	Baptist	Fullerton, CA
Huebert, Frank D.	Mennonite General Conference	Frazer, MT

Name	Denomination	Drafted From
Hulvey, Oscar M.	Brethren	Mount Sidney, VA
Hulvey, Paul C.	Brethren	Mount Sidney, VA
Hunter, Dwight D.	Jehovah's Witness	Modesto, CA
Ikenberry, Ellis E.	Brethren	Overbrook, KS
Illick, Paul E.	Methodist	Syracuse, NY
Isely, H. Philip	None	Salem, OR
Iten, George J.	Assembly of God	Burbank, CA
Jackson, Leon Klamath	None	Beatty, OR
Jaderborg, Einar H.	Lutheran	Lindsborg, KS
Jadiker, William V.	None	Los Angeles, CA
Jahn, John P.	Congregational Christian	Berkeley, CA
Jantz, Franklin D.	Mennonite Church of God in Christ	Livingston, CA
Jehnzen, Charles G.	Brethren	Rodney, MI
Johnson, Douglas R.	None	Yellow Springs, OH
Johnson, George A.	None	Los Angeles, CA
Johnson, Louis R.	Brethren	Modesto, CA
Johnson, R. Norman	Brethren	East Modesto, CA
Johnson, Robert	Congregational Christian	Portland, OR
Johnson, Roger K.	Methodist	Portland, OR
Johnson, Roy V.	None	Tacoma, WA
Johnson, Theodore R.	Methodist	Los Angeles, CA
Jones, Denver E.	Brethren	Cerro Gordo, IL
Jones, Lyle L.	Brethren	Wetonka, SD
Jost, Arthur	Mennonite Brethren	Fresno, CA
Jovanovich, John A.	Serbian Orthodox	Fresno, CA
Keeton, Kenneth H.	Methodist	Elgin, IL
Keller, James E.	Brethren	Oak Park, IL
Kenworthy, Melvin W.	Friend	Portland, OR
Kerr, Edmund J.	Presbyterian	Phoenix, AZ
Kessler, Denver E.	Brethren	Cerro Gordo, IL
Kessler, Warren H.	Brethren	Meridian, ID
Ketner, Willard P.	Jehovah's Witness	Sylvan, WA
Kidder, Eugene F.	Methodist	Lynwood, CA
Kimmel, Kenneth S.	Brethren	Lawrence, KS
Kindy, Paul E.	Brethren	Middlebury, IN
King, Leonard J.	Mennonite	Wauseon, OH
Kintner, Emery B.	Brethren	Bryan, OH
Kirschner, H. Don	Disciples of Christ	Beatrice, NE
Kleiner, Harold A.	Methodist	Portland, OR
Kline, Jack	Brethren	Sidney, OH
Klingenberg, Clarence E.	Mennonite	Bakersfield, CA
Knapp, Charles L.	Jehovah's Witness	Burns, OR

Name	Denomination	Drafted From
Koenig, Richard C.	Evangelical & Reformed	Chicago, IL
Koepl, Albert	Unitarian	Springfield, OR
Koepl, Aloysius N.	Unitarian	Springfield, OR
Koepl, Leo J.	Unitarian	Springfield, OR
Kolhoff, Kenneth M.	Brethren	Pasadena, CA
Kozelisky, Joseph A.	Jehovah's Witness	Ronald, WA
Krabill, David C.	Mennonite Old	Albany, OR
Krhen, John R.	Jehovah's Witness	Tarzana, CA
Kropf, Harry L.	Mennonite	Halsey, OR
Kropf, Lester S.	Mennonite Old	Hubbard, OR
Krug, Lyle F.	Mennonite General Conference	Silverton, OR
Lahman, George W.	German Baptist	Modesto, CA
Lammadee, Alva D.	Brethren	Tacoma, WA
Land, John E.	Christadelphian	Chino, CA
Landis, Jason C.	Mennonite	Lancaster, PA
Langford, R. Victor	Presbyterian	San Marino, CA
Larrew, Lloyd H.	Mennonite Old	Blaine, OR
Lawber, William L.	Brethren	Nampa, ID
Leasure, Fred	Brethren	Manchester, IN
Leasure, Melvin	Brethren	Manchester, IN
Leedy, Eugene A.	Brethren	Lima, OH
Leedy, Kenneth D.	Brethren	Lima, OH
Lehman, Rodney L.	Brethren	Glendora, CA
Lehrman, Melvin C.	Mennonite General Conference	Brooks, OR
Levig, Donald E.	Community Church	Port Angeles, WA
Lewis, Elmer C.	Friend	Newberg, OR
Lewis, Francis R.	Methodist	Seattle, WA
Lichti, Rudolph	Mennonite General Conference	Parlier, CA
Lindsey, David	None	Lancaster, PA
Liskey, Samuel W.	None	Pomona CA
Little, Jesse F.	Church of God	Philadelphia, PA
Lornell, Wallace M.	Lutheran	Minneapolis, MN
Loscutloff, John	Russian Molokan	San Francisco, CA
Lowber, William Lincoln (Dub)	Brethren	Nampa, ID
Magee, John L.	Methodist	Dayton, OH
Mahin, Charles	Brethren	West Los Angeles, CA
Mammone, Nicholas	Christadelphian	Jersey City, NJ
Markley, Leland E.	Brethren	Elkhart, IN
Marsh, LeRoy N.	Jehovah's Witness	Big Fort, MT
Martin, Carl S.	Brethren in Christ	Chambersburg, PA

Name	Denomination	Drafted From
Martin, James A.	Presbyterian	Portland, OR
Martin, Leslie B.	Brethren	Reno, NV
Martin, Robert L.	Methodist	Seattle, WA
Marzolf, Philip	Baptist	Martin, ND
Mason, Carroll H.	Brethren	Broadway, VA
Mason, George E.	Methodist	Gardena, CA
Mason, John R.	Brethren	Bassett, VA
Mason, Olin J.	Brethren	Bridgewater, VA
Maurer, George P.	Methodist	Los Angeles, CA
McCaffree, Joe E.	Lemurian Fellowship	Los Angeles, CA
McCray, Jack C.	Brethren	Chico, CA
McCullough, William B.	None	Tacoma, WA
McGinnis, Robert S.	Jehovah's Witness	Portland, OR
McIntyre, Ross L.	Friend	Caldwell, ID
McKinney, George B.	Assembly of God	Los Angeles, CA
McLane, Robert	Methodist	Chico, CA
McMurrin, James I.	Church of God	St. Joe, AR
McNutt, Earl F.	Brethren	Mount Morris, IL
McRae, Alan B.	Congregational Christian	Seattle, WA
McReynolds, William	None	Salem, OR
Meeks, Benton G.	Methodist	Cleveland, OH
Merrick, Hugh *see* Forsyth, Brian		
Michael, Herbert	Brethren	Bagley, IA
Miller Alvin W.	None	Monterey Park, CA
Miller, Delbert F.	Brethren	Wenatchee, WA
Miller, Joseph W.	Holiness	Barnsdall, OK
Miller, Kenneth R.	Brethren	Beatrice, NE
Miller, Noble S.	Nazarene	Ochelata, OK
Miller, Robert L.	Brethren	Beatrice, NE
Miller, Tom Polk	None	Houston, TX
Mills, Richard C.	Congregational	Los Angeles, CA
Minear, Floyd L.	Brethren	Ashland, OR
Miner, Dana L.	Swedish Mission Covenant	Cascade Locks, OR
Minnich, Charles Otto	Brethren	Pomona, CA
Mitaraky, John	Greek Orthodox	Chicago, IL
Mohler, Daniel W.	German Baptist	Ripon, CA
Monson, Melton A.	None	Glenwood City, WI
Morgan, Lawrence	Disciples of Christ	Opportunity, WA
Morton, Russell A.	Nazarene	Nampa, ID
Mueller Grant A.	Congregational Christian	Seattle, WA
Mulkey, Jack M.	Brethren	Myrtle Point, OR
Mullinix, Samuel E.	Methodist	Mount Airy, MD

Name	Denomination	Drafted From
Myers, Delbert L.	Jehovah's Witness	Cottage Grove, OR
Myers, William	Brethren	Hollywood, CA
Myers, Worth	None	Pico, CA
Nafziger, William Edgar	Mennonite	Salem, OR
Nash, Stanley W.	Evangelical	Tieton, WA
Neufeld, Frank E.	Mennonite Brethren	Dinuba, CA
Neumann, Louis P.	Congregational Christian	Glendora, CA
Nickel, Clarence L.	Mennonite General Conference	Salem, OR
Nofziger, Morris E.	Mennonite	Lebanon, OR
Nolt, Melville T.	Brethren	Akron, OH
Nomland, Kemper	None	Los Angeles, CA
Nunnally, Bill O.	Church of Christ	Memphis, TN
Nunnally, J. B.	Church of Christ	Memphis, TN
Nusbaum, Lawrence E.	Brethren	Goshen, IN
Nyce, William P.	Brethren	Lansdale, PA
Oden, LeRoy	Jehovah's Witness	Llano, CA
O'Kelley, Dallas T.	Christadelphian	Conway, AR
Olin, Bertel J.	Lutheran	Eugene, OR
Olsen, Roy H.	Assembly of God	Molalla, OR
Olson, Glen E.	None	Camerton, MT
Orcutt, Albert W.	Presbyterian	Huntington Park, CA
Orser, Dave A.	Methodist	Amherst, VA
Ortmayer, Roland L.	Methodist	Glendive, MT
Paine, Wayne C.	The Lord Our Righteousness	Cle Elum, WA
Palmer, John Ralph	Friend	Nampa ID
Parker James	Christadelphian	Los Angeles, CA
Parks, William C.	Brethren	Shippensburg, PA
Pearson, Wilfred D.	Friend	Portland, OR
Peaster, Marvin	Mennonite Church of God in Christ	Winton, CA
Pederson, Edgar	None	Seattle, WA
Penney, Aubrey J.	Plymouth Brethren	Los Angeles, CA
Perkins, Richard T.	Church of God	Washington, DC
Peterson, Pritchard J.	Brethren	Mountain Grove, MO
Phillips, James C.	Christadelphian	Canton, OH
Phillips, William A.	Presbyterian	Los Angeles, CA
Picone, Vincent E.	Methodist	Chicago, IL
Pobst, Galen B.	Brethren	Leavenworth, KS
Porter, Eugene C.	Jehovah's Witness	Kindrick, ID
Portnoff, William P.	Russian Molokan	Bakersfield, CA
Potochnik, Rudy A.	None	Detroit, MI
Pottenger, Hal W.	Methodist	Warsaw, IN

Name	Denomination	Drafted From
Powell, Roland R.	Jehovah's Witness	Los Angeles, CA
Pratt, L. Laurence	Methodist	Eugene, OR
Price, Claude	Disciples of Christ	Bremerton, WA
Prochaska, Harry	None	Monterey Park, CA
Prough, William W.	Jehovah's Witness	Klamath Falls, OR
Pyper. William J.	Brethren	Tonasket, WA
Quiring, Jacob R.	Mennonite Brethren	Los Angeles, CA
Ragsdale, Randolph H.	None	Pomona, CA
Redfield, Donald E.	Methodist	Burley, ID
Reed, Dean F.	Brethren	Galesburg, KS
Reeser, Harvey W.	Mennonite Old	Albany, OR
Regier, John H.	Mennonite Brethren	Reedley, CA
Reish, William E.	Brethren	Christiansburg, VA
Reynolds, Carl B.	Jehovah's Witness	Arvin, CA
Richardson, Donald N.	Evangelical Christian	New Leipzig, ND
Richert, Julius	Congregational Christian	Fresno, CA
Richwine, Calvin A.	Brethren	Froid, MT
Riggins, Floyd F.	Jehovah's Witness	Summerville, OR
Rinehart, Warren L.	Brethren	Modesto, CA
Roark, Floyd F.	None	Priest River, ID
Robbins, Guy Thomas	Methodist	San Rafael, CA
Roberson, Charles E.	Church of Christ	Nashville, TN
Roberts, Delbert Ellis	Friend	Wallingford, PA
Roberts, Donald M.	Methodist	Alhambra, CA
Roberts, F. David	None	Seattle, WA
Roberts, Ray Clayton	None	Seattle, WA
Rogers, Maurice A.	Jehovah's Witness	Bakersfield, CA
Rohbock, Frank	Latter Day Saints	Provo, UT
Rohrer, Glenn N.	Brethren	Wabash, IN
Romaine, Richard N.	Jehovah's Witness	Tacoma, WA
Root, Fred V.	Brethren	LaVerne, CA
Root, John Allen	Old German Baptist	Empire, CA
Roslie, Joseph	Jehovah's Witness	Tacoma, WA
Ross, C. Marion	Brethren	Laton, CA
Roth, Menno	Mennonite Old	Sweet Home, OR
Rothman, Sanford D.	Jewish	Los Angeles, CA
Rouddeau, Leo A.	Catholic	White Bluffs, WA
Royer, Clarence J.	Brethren	Palms, CA
Rozeboom, Gerrit A.	Methodist	Sebastopol, CA
Rubin, Gerald M.	Jewish	San Francisco, CA
Ruff, Wilbur L.	Brethren	Yakima, WA
Rutschman, Roy	Mennonite	Silverton, OR
Sapp, Clarence	Methodist	Boise, ID
Schaad, Loyd O.	Methodist	Newberg, OR

Name	Denomination	Drafted From
Schaeffer, Joseph P.	Catholic	Philadelphia, PA
Schimanski, Hans	None	Colbert, WA
Schipper, William	Jehovah's Witness	San Pedro, CA
Schmidt, Andrew E.	Mennonite Evangelical Brethren	Lustre, MT
Schmidt, Peter E.	Mennonite Evangelical Brethren	Lustre, MT
Schmucker, Isaac L.	Brethren	Nappanee, IN
Schrock, Manassa	Mennonite Old	Sheridan, OR
Scott, Robert H.	Brethren	Long Beach, CA
Scott, Victor F.	Evangelistic Mission	East Lansing, MI
Scroggins, Cleo L.	Jehovah's Witness	Cottage Grove, OR
Searles, Robert C.	Methodist	Tacoma, WA
Shaffer, Alvin C.	Brethren	Denton, MD
Sheets, Kermit	Baptist	Fresno, CA
Sherman, Charles W.	Brethren	McVey Town, PA
Sherman, Russell F.	Brethren	Henderson, PA
Shilling, Merle Kenneth	Brethren	Johnstown, PA
Showalter, Kenneth G.	Brethren	Canton, OH
Shubin, Morris J.	Russian Molokan	Los Angeles, CA
Siebert, Walter F.	Mennonite General Conference	Henderson, NE
Silvers, Orlan D.	German Baptist	Los Angeles, CA
Sisk, Ralph L.	Congregational Christian	Modesto, CA
Smith, David S.	Methodist	Rupert, ID
Smith, Donald Elton	Brethren	Artesia, CA
Smith, J. Wesley	Community Church	Portland, OR
Smith, Norman O.	Methodist	Portland, OR
Smith, Otto B.	Church of Christ	Saugus, CA
Smith, Raymond H.	Jehovah's Witness	Redmond, WA
Smith, Victor	Jehovah's Witness	Glasgow Valley, MT
Spear, Virgil M.	Brethren	Cedar Rapids, IA
Spear, Wilmer E.	Brethren	Cedar Rapids, IA
St. Luise, Christopher	None	Chelan, WA
Stanley Don E.	Friend	Whittier, CA
Steckly, Allen C.	Mennonite	Albany, OR
Stefan, Walter	Evangelical & Reformed	Chicago Heights, IL
Steinberger, Kenneth L.	Brethren	Delano, CA
Stewart, David D.	Methodist	Berkeley, CA
Stout, Raymond A.	Dunkard Brethren	Wabash, IN
Stover, Lloyd E.	Brethren	Garden City, KS
Strain, Douglas	Church of God Seventh Day	Portland, OR

Name	Denomination	Drafted From
Strubhar, Levi A.	Mennonite Old	Hubbard, OR
Strubhar, Timothy J.	Mennonite Old	Hubbard, OR
Stutzman, Daniel E.	Mennonite	Halsey, OR
Sutton, Sewell	Brethren	Hillsboro, OH
Switzer, Roscoe D.	Brethren	Mankato, KS
Tate, John W.	Brethren	Salem, VA
Taylor, Charles G.	Brethren	Glasgow, MT
Taylor, James E.	Baptist	Glasgow, MT
Taylor, Wendell F.	Disciples of Christ	Monroe, WA
Ten Brink, Howard	Methodist	Spring Green, WI
Thiesen, Milton J.	Mennonite Brethren	Dinuba, CA
Thiessen, Leonard	Mennonite Brethren	Dinuba, CA
Thornton, Leonard L.	Jehovah's Witness	Glasgow Valley, MT
Tittle, William M.	Methodist	Evanston, IL
Toews, Abe A.	Mennonite Brethren	Frazer, MT
Toothaker, William F.	Methodist	Oakland, CA
Torkelson, Arthur R.	Mennonite Old	Sweet Home, OR
Towle, Delwin	Jehovah's Witness	Seattle, WA
Townsend, James E.	None	San Francisco, CA
Trostle, John B.	Brethren	Nickerson, KS
Trumbo, Harold A.	Brethren	Fulks Run, VA
Trumbo, Olliver O.	Brethren	Fulks Run, VA
Tuinstra, George R.	None	Corvalllis, OR
Tuttle, George Richard	Methodist	Aberdeen, WA
Twet, Omer S.	Lutheran	Portland, OR
Unruh, Lawrence W.	Mennonite Church of God in Christ	Upland, CA
Upperman, Carl E.	Christian Science	Palo Alto, CA
Utley, Windsor R.	None	New York, NY
Vanderburg, Raymond L.	Methodist	Fullerton, CA
Vaniman, Delbert N.	Brethren	Ventura, CA
Velasquez, Juan	Church of God	Bay City, MI
Verbeck, Raymond L.	Brethren	Wenatchee, WA
Verduin, Carl H.	Reformed Church	Chicago Heights, IL
Vice, Charles F.	Brethren	Durham, CA
Vice, David R.	Brethren	Durham, CA
Villa, Arthur D.	Pentecostal	El Monte, CA
Wadsworth, Paul S.	Jehovah's Witness	Pasadena, CA
Wagoner, Jesse E.	Old German Baptist	Modesto, CA
Warkentin, Ervin Johnnie	Mennonite Brethren	Reedley, CA
Washburn, James A.	Methodist	Caldwell, ID
Weaver, Edgar M.	Baptist	Napa, CA
Weaver, John S.	Congregational Christian	Clinton, MI
Weaver, Raymond C.	Brethren	Waterford, CA

Name	Denomination	Drafted From
Webb, William	None	Los Angeles, CA
Weber, William A.	Congregational Christian	Pullman, WA
Weimer, Kenneth E.	Brethren	Modesto, CA
Welch, Sydney R.	Brethren	Modesto, CA
Wells II, George S.	Friend	Washington, DC
Werner, George Albert	Brethren	Lineboro, MD
Whistleman, Fred C.	Brethren	Greenville, VA
Whitmer, Amos A.	Brethren	LaVerne, CA
Wickline, Willard Cecil	Methodist	Warrenton, OR
Wiebe, Leonard	Mennonite General Conference	Upland, CA
Wiens, Edward	Mennonite Brethren	Winton, CA
Wilder, Robert E.	Jehovah's Witness	Eugene, OR
Wilkins, Melvin L.	Friend	Newberg, OR
Williams, Floyd Wendell	Friend	Greenleaf, ID
Williams, Owen	Christadelphian	Yoakum, TX
Winker, James B.	Methodist	Portland, OR
Wolf, Arthur	German Baptist	Modesto, CA
Wolf, Joseph J.	German Baptist	Modesto, CA
Wood, Robert R.	Evangelical	Mapleton Ranger Station, OR
Woodward, Frank L.	Brethren	Tacoma, WA
Worthington, James P.	Brethren	Artesia, CA
Wulf, Immo W.	Christian Scientist	Detroit, MI
Xavier, Felix G.	Father Divine	Tacoma, WA
Yamada, George H.	Evangelical & Reformed	San Francisco, CA
Yearout, Robert L.	Brethren	Fresno, CA
Yerden, Maurice R.	Church of God	Alegan, MI
Yoder, Ammon	Mennonite Conservative Amish	Harrisburg, OR
Yoder, Jay Warren	Mennonite	West Liberty, OH
Yoder, Robert D.	Mennonite Old	Hillsboro, OR
Yost, Harold K.	Mennonite Old	Atwater, CA
Zook, Loren E.	Brethren	Whittier, CA

NOTES & BIBLIOGRAPHY

List of Abbreviations

Brethren Brethren Historical Library and Archives, Elgin, Illinois.
Bridgewater Alexander Mack Library, Bridgewater College, Bridgewater, Virginia.
Davis-Kovac The Charles Davis-Jeffrey Kovac Collection.
LC Blocher / LC Schrock / LC Sheets / LC Stafford The Henry & Mary Blocher
   Collection, the Julian Schrock Collection, the Kermit Sheets Collection, and the
   William Stafford Archives, Lewis & Clark College, Portland, Oregon.

Foreword

1. This quote appears as the frontispiece to Heisey, *Peace Persistence.*

Chapter One

1. Kennedy, *Freedom From Fear*, 632-34.
2. Brock and Young, *Pacifism in the Twentieth Century*, 17.
3. Sibley and Jacob, *Conscription of Conscience.*
4. Eisan, *Pathways of Peace*; Melvin Gingerich, *Service for Peace.*
5. Sibley and Jacob, *Conscription of Conscience.*
6. Wachs, "Conscription, Conscientious Objection, and the Context of American
   Pacifism, 1940-1945."
7. Robinson, "Civilian Public Service during World War II: The Dilemmas of
   Conscience and Conscription in a Free Society."
8. Keim, *The CPS Story.*
9. Saryan, *The Turning Point.*
10. Tucker, *The Great Starvation Experiment.*
11. Matthews, *Smoke Jumping on the Western Fire Line.*
12. For example, Stafford, *Down in My Heart*; Dasenbrock, *To the Beat of a Different
   Drummer*; Smith, *Six Year Passage*; Joe Nunnaly, *I Was a Conscientious Objector.*
13. Eller, *Conscientious Objectors and the Second World War*; Frazier and O'Sullivan,
   *We Have Just Begun to Not Fight; Camp 56: An Oral History Project, World War
   II Conscientious Objectors and the Waldport, Oregon Civilian Public Service Camp.*
   http://www.ccrh.org/oral/co.pdf (accessed November 13, 2007); "The CO
   Project," http://speak4peace.com/thecoproject.html (accessed November 13,
   2007).
14. Anderson, *Peace Was In Their Hearts.*
15. Goossen, *Women Against the Good War.*
16. http://www.pbs.org/itvs/thegoodwar/ (accessed March 13, 2008).
17. http://www.pbs.org/itvs/thegoodwar/GW_transcript.pdf, p. 9 (accessed
   March 13, 2008).
18. Letter from Don Smith to the author, March 6, 2008. Davis-Kovac.
19. Orser, "Involuntary Community: Conscientious Objectors at Patapsco State
   Park During World War II."
20. Zahn, *Another Side of War: The Camp Simon Story.*
21. Sibley and Jacob, *Conscription of Conscience*, 68.
22. NIBSCO, *1996 Directory of Civilian Public Service.* Washington, DC: NIBSCO,
   1996, Appendix D, xxii-xxix.
23. "21 One of Most Significant Camps — Row." *Columbian* 1:13 (July 10, 1942), 2.

24. Letter from Howard Hamilton to Harold Row and Ora Houston, August 3, 1946. Brethren. Copy in Davis-Kovac.
25. Grimsrud, "An Ethical Analysis of Conscientious Objection to World War II."
26. Ibid., 21.
27. Brock and Young, *Pacifism in the Twentieth Century*, 135.
28. Sibley and Jacob, *Conscription of Conscience*.
29. Robinson, "Civilian Public Service during World War II."
30. The records of CPS #21 and all other camps operated by the Brethren Service Committee are preserved primarily on microfilm at the Brethren Historical Library and Archives in Elgin, Ill. These archives also contain print copies of various camp newspapers and collections of photographs.
31. The mimeographed documents comprising the history of CPS #21 are in the possession of the author courtesy of Don Elton Smith.
32. Schrock, *At Cascade Locks*. A copy is in the author's files courtesy of Julian Schrock.
33. "Footprints of Pacifism: The Creative Lives of Kemper Nomland and Kermit Sheets." http://digitalcollections.lclark.edu/cgi-bin/showfile. exe?CISOROOT=/pubs&CISOPTR=41 (accessed November 14, 2007).
34. I am grateful to Harold Bock for providing these copies. Davis-Kovac.
35. DVD copies of these interviews are in the possession of the author. Davis-Kovac. Also at LC.
36. Keegan, *A History of Warfare*, 385.

Chapter Two

1. Sibley and Jacob, *Conscription of Conscience*, 10-16; Keim and Stoltzfus, *The Politics of Conscience*, ch. 2; Homan, *American Mennonites and the Great War: 1914-1918*.
2. Sibley and Jacob, *Conscription of Conscience*, 14-15; Cooney and Michalowski, eds., *The Power of the People*, 44-45; Kraybill and Bowman, *On the Backroad to Heaven: Old Order Hutterites,Mennonites, Amish, and Brethren*, 30; Homan, *American Mennonites and the Great War.*
3. Quoted in Keim and Stotzfus, *The Politics of Conscience*, 52.
4. Eisan, *Pathways of Peace*, ch. 13.
5. Frazer and O'Sullivan, *We Have Just Begun to Not Fight*, 231.
6. Ibid., 232.
7. "About Morris Keeton," http://www.umuc.edu/odell/irahe/morris.html (accessed February 8, 2007).
8. M. R. Zigler to Kermit Sheets, December 12, 1941. LC Sheets. Copy in Davis-Kovac.

Chapter Three

1. Dasenbrock, *To the Beat of a Different Drummer*, ch. 2.
2. Schrock, *At Cascade Locks*.
3. Schrock, "The First Seven Weeks in CPS Camp No. 21." Davis-Kovac.
4. Quoted in Dasenbrock, *To the Beat of a Different Drummer*, 28.
5. Harry Prochaska, "History of CPS #21: Art Activities in CPS #21." Don Elton Smith papers in Davis-Kovac.
6. Dasenbrock, *To the Beat of a Different Drummer*, 36. Schrock, *At Cascade Locks*. The Blocher photos are at LC.

7. Dasenbrock, *To the Beat of a Different Drummer,* 40.

8. Schrock, *At Cascade Locks.*

9. Richard Anderson to the author, July 24, 2006. Davis-Kovac.

10. Harland Gibson, interview with author, Sacramento, Calif., August 2007.

11. Schrock, *At Cascade Locks.*

12. Charles Davis to family and friends, July 11, 1942. Davis-Kovac.

13. Ibid.

14. Interview with Don Elton Smith, Loveland, Colo., July 16, 2007.

15. Ibid. Don Smith did not know who put the sign on the footlocker, but it might well have been Charlie Davis.

16. Charles Davis, "Varied Tasks Comprise Camp Work, Program." *Columbian* 1:1 (January 30, 1942), 3.

17. Kenneth Keeton and Don Elton Smith, "History of CPS #21: The Work Project, and Related Problems Caused by Differing Viewpoints." August 1945. Don Elton Smith papers in Davis-Kovac.

18. *Columbian* 1: 1 (January 30, 1942).

19. Schrock, *At Cascade Locks.*

20. Interview with Don Baker, San Francisco, Calif., August 7, 2007.

21. Don Elton Smith, "Development of Techniques of Administration in CPS #21." November 15, 1944. Don Elton Smith papers in Davis-Kovac.

22. "ULV to Honor Dwight Hanawalt, Commemorate Old Gym with Tribute Event on May 16." http://www.ulv.edu/ur/press/show.phtml?id=359 (accessed October 17, 2007).

23. Lee, *A Passion for Quality,* 2-3.

24. Les Abbenhouse, "Camp Store Operates on Co-op Principles." *Columbian* 1: 6 (March 28, 1942), 6.

25. Principles of the Rochdale Cooperative. http://uts.cc.utexas.edu/~laurel/cooproots/principle.html (accessed January 27, 2007).

26. "Camp Launches Farm Project." *Columbian* 1: 5 (March 28, 1942).

27. Mark Schrock to Harold Row regarding the quality and quantity of food served in Brethren CPS Camps, October 4, 1943. Davis-Kovac.

28. George Wells, "Men Fight Season's First Fire." *Columbian* 1: 6 (April 11, 1942).

29. Lew Ayres, "My Stand for Conscientious Objection." Davis-Kovac.

30. "Lew Ayres Is a Conscientious Objector: His First Major Role was in Anti-War Film." *New York Times,* March 31, 1942, 23.

31. Schrock, *At Cascade Locks.*

32. Stewart-Winter, "Not a Soldier, Not a Slacker."

33. "Lew Ayres." *Washington Post,* April 5, 1942.

34. Frost, "Conscientious Objection and Popular Culture: The Case of Lew Ayres."

35. "Lew Ayres." *Columbian* 1: 9 (May 23, 1942), 1-2.

36. "Ayres to Medical Unit from Objectors' Camp." *New York Times* May 18, 1942, 18.

37. "Lew Ayres," *Columbian* 1: 9 (May 23, 1942), 1-2.

38. I am indebted to Richard Anderson for these insights about the relationship between Lew Ayres and Mark Schrock. Richard Anderson to the author, December 22, 2006. Davis-Kovac.

39. Lew Ayres to Mark Schrock, August 18, 1942. Davis-Kovac.

40. Mark Schrock to Lew Ayres, April 22, 1943. Davis-Kovac.

41. http://www.pbs.org/itvs/thegood war/field.html. (accessed December 12, 2006).
42. Ayres, *Altars of the East.*
43. "Lew Ayres." *Columbian* 1: 9 (May 23, 1942), 1-2.
44. Charles Davis, personal communication.
45. "Col. Kosch," *Columbian* 1: 7 (April 24, 1942), 3.

Chapter Four

1. Harmon, *They Also Serve.*
2. "Hospital Units," *Columbian* 1: 7 (April 24, 1942), 1; "Salem Hospital," *Columbian* 1: 8 (May 9, 1942), 1.
3. "Legion, Labor Protests Defeat Hospital Unit." *Columbian* 1: 11 (June 20, 1942), 2.
4. Brock and Young, *Pacifism in the Twentieth Century*, 101-102.
5. "FOR Group Forms," *Columbian* 1: 8 (May 9, 1942), 1.
6. "Socialists State Policy," *Columbian* 1: 9 (May 23, 1942), 5.
7. Harold Row to Mark Schrock, June 3, 1942. Brethren. Copy in Davis-Kovac.
8. Mark Schrock to Harold Row, June 10, 1942. Brethren. Copy in Davis-Kovac.
9. Schrock, *At Cascade Locks.*
10. Ed Kerr, "Summer Vacation Section: Mud Lake," *Columbian* 1: 14 (August 1, 1942).
11. "Commutation Plea Phoned to Virginia Governor," *Columbian* 1: 11 (June 20, 1942).
12. E. W. Rise, Review of *The Case of Odell Waller and Virginia Justice, 1940-1942*, by Richard B. Sherman. *Journal of Southern History* 60 (1994), 167-8.
13. George Yamada, "My Story of World War II," in Gara and Gara, *A Few Small Candles*, 194-204.
14. tenBroek, Barnhart and Matson, *Prejudice, War and the Constitution,* 100-101.
15. Ibid., 110.
16. Individual persons of Italian or German descent were apprehended, but there was no mass removal and incarceration of either of these populations.
17. tenBroek, Barnhart and Matson, *Prejudice, War and the Constitution,* 202.
18. The exact date this telegram was received by Mark Schrock is unknown, but it was certainly on or before June 29, 1942, and may have been as early as June 21. It is likely that Schrock would have spent some time talking with Yamada and others whom he trusted before making a general announcement. The text was reproduced in a letter sent by the members of CPS #21 to other camps. An entry in the diary of camp member, Richard C. Anderson dated May 31, 1942 indicates that George Yamada knew as early as April that he would be ordered to leave the camp. According to Anderson, Yamada had been told by Colonel Kosch, who had visited the camp in April, that he would have to leave and go to some other camp in the inland of the country. At the time of his conversation with Anderson, Yamada was beginning to think about his best course of action. The relevant parts of Anderson's diary were sent to Charles Davis on February 18, 1989, and are in the Davis-Kovac Collection.
19. The text quoted is taken from a copy of a letter from Mark Schrock to W. Harold Row contained in the Davis files. Excerpts from the letter appeared in the July 4, 1942 issue of *The Columbian* (issue 1: 12).
20. The source for the chronology was the private diary of Lloyd A. Hall. Copies of the relevant pages were sent to Charles Davis by Dr. Hall on June 29, 1989,

and are in the Davis-Kovac Collection. Additional details came from the Richard Anderson diary.

21. Hurwitz and Simpson, *Against the Tide*, 40.
22. Note by Charles Davis appended to a photocopy of George Brown's obituary from the *New York Times*. Davis-Kovac.
23. Education Report, July 1942, Brethren. Copy in Davis-Kovac.
24. "CPS Camps Protest Evacuation of Yamada," *Columbian*, 1: 12 (July 4, 1942), 4.
25. An original mimeograph copy of this letter is in the Davis-Kovac Collection. The text was also published in the July 4, 1942 issue of *The Columbian* (1: 12), 1.
26. For a further discussion of the influence of Gandhian philosophy on COs see Sibley and Jacob, *Conscription of Conscience*, especially chapters 2 and 18.
27. An airmail letter dated July 6, 1942 from camp president Charles Davis to other CPS camps and interested persons contains excerpts from nine supporting telegrams that had been received. Many of these excerpts indicate that telegrams have been sent to either General Hershey or Colonel Bendetsen, or both. Other telegrams might have been received, but I have not found a complete collection or list. A copy of this letter is in the Davis-Kovac Collection.
28. Richard C. Mills, "A Report of the Proposed Discharge of George Yamada from CPS Camp #21," undated. Brethren. Copy in Davis-Kovac.
29. An original mimeograph copy of this letter dated July 21, 1942, is in the Davis-Kovac Collection.
30. Sibley and Jacob, *Conscription of Conscience*, 312-13. These pages provide a fuller discussion of the positions of the three denominations.
31. See Sibley and Jacob, *Conscription of Conscience*, chapter 8 for a fuller discussion. The oral histories related in Gara and Gara, *A Few Small Candles* are primarily those of activist COs. Another source is Tracy, *Direct Action*.
32. Dasenbrock, *To the Beat of A Different Drummer*, 38-9.
33. The details of these three cases can be found in Irons, *Justice at War*.
34. Richard Anderson's diary entry for July 4, 1942. Davis-Kovac.
35. The Paul Comly French Diary in the Swarthmore College Peace Collection is a restricted document that can be accessed only with the permission of the Center on Conscience and War, the successor to NSBRO. The relevant pages are in the Davis files and are used by permission.
36. Richard Anderson diary. Davis-Kovac.
37. deNevers, *The Colonel and the Pacifist*, 134, 138-40.
38. See Robinson, "Civilian Public Service During World War II," especially chapter 7.
39. The anger of the Selective Service administration was long lived. On September 7, 1943 W. Harold Row wrote to Mark Schrock to inform him of an unfavorable report on Cascade Locks by Col. McLean. Row had also talked with Col. Kosch, who himself had negative things to say about Schrock. As an explanation, Row writes, "Apparently they have not forgotten the Yamada case." Row's letters, however, indicate strong personal support for both Schrock and Charlie Davis. Both letters are in Davis-Kovac.
40. Row's remarks to the camp are reported in detail in Richard Anderson's diary entry for July 6, 1942. Davis-Kovac.
41. Eisan, *Pathways of Peace*, 47.
42. My perspective on Mark Schrock has been enriched by reading Julian Schrock's personal memoir of Cascade Locks, and by telephone conversations

with surviving members of CPS #21 and with Mae Henderson, who was Mark Schrock's volunteer secretary at his church in Olympia and married Bill Henderson, a CO who spent some time at CPS #21.

43. Schrock, *At Cascade Locks.*

44. Charles Davis to Colonel Lewis F. Kosch, July 9, 1942. Davis-Kovac.

45. The letter, signed by Charles Davis as Camp President, is in the Davis files. It was also published in the July 7, 1942 issue of *The Columbian* (1: 12). This issue was a supplement to the July 4, 1942 issue. In a letter to Charles Davis dated March 24, 1989, George Yamada suggests that this statement was actually written by someone else to provide an explanation. Yamada adds that he was not really prepared for the role that was thrust upon him. This letter is in the Davis-Kovac Collection.

46. This handwritten letter dated August 6, 1942, is in the files of Mark Schrock and was kindly provided by Julian Schrock. Copy in Davis-Kovac.

47. George Yamada, in Gara and Gara, *A Few Small Candles.*

48. Eisan, *Pathways of Peace,* 47.

49. "Hospital Unit Opens," *Columbian* 1: 15 (August 15, 1942), 1-2.

50. "Tobey, Mark (1890-1976): The Old Master of the Young American Painting," Historylink.org: The Free Online Encyclopedia of Washington State History, http://www.historylink.org/index.cfm?DisplayPage=output.cfm&File_Id=5217 (accessed November 4, 2008).

51. http://www.fosterwhite.com/dynamic/artist.asp?ArtistID=24; http://www.vashonislandfineart.com/windsor_utley.htm (accessed November 4, 2008).

52. Mark Schrock to Harold Row, May 11, 1942. Brethren. Copy in Davis-Kovac.

53. "BSC Appoints Mills Assistant Director," *Columbian* 1: 13 (July 18, 1942), 8.

54. Mark Schrock to Harold Row, October 2, 1942. Brethren Archives. The Archives also included an undated typescript of the article from *The Oregon Journal.* The quotations from the *Oregonian* and from the Handsaker letter were found in an unsigned document, "The Clackamas River Project," in LC Sheets. Copies of these documents are in Davis-Kovac.

55. "Excerpts from a Discussion of the Three Lynx Project on the Clackamas River by James Frankland, Regional Engineer, and Jack Horton, Regional Office." Brethren. Copy in Davis-Kovac.

56. This information comes from pages of a diary kept by Joe Gunterman in LC Sheets. Gunterman's diary spans the period October-December 1942, and includes copies of letters sent to Paul Comly French and Mark Schrock as well as Schrock's response. Copy in Davis-Kovac.

57. An unsigned handwritten letter to Mark Schrock from Three Lynx dated December 15, 1942 was found in the CPS 21 papers in the Brethren Archives. This letter discusses the current work of the crew: putting up buildings. Copy in Davis-Kovac.

58. A copy of the petition dated October 10, 1942 was found in camp records in the Brethren Archives. Copy in Davis-Kovac.

59. Joe Gunterman diary. Davis-Kovac.

60. I am indebted to Don Elton Smith for this insight into the various stands of COs at Cascade Locks. Don Smith to the author, October 24, 2006. Davis-Kovac.

61. Joe Gunterman diary. Davis-Kovac.

62. Mark Schrock to Frank Rypczynski, November 9, 1942. Davis-Kovac.

63. Mark Schrock to Harold Row, November 9, 1942. Davis-Kovac.
64. Mark Schrock to Bill Cable, November 2, 1942. Davis-Kovac.
65. Mark Schrock to Frank Rypczyski, November 10, 1942. Davis-Kovac.
66. This exchange of letters is reproduced in Bowman, "An Historical and Interpretive Study of the Church of the Brethren and War," 378-9.
67. Bowman, 379; Joe Gunterman diary, Davis-Kovac.
68. The full statement can be found in Bowman's dissertation.

Chapter Six

1. *Columbian* 1: 18 (February 1943), 1.
2. Schrock, *At Cascade Locks.*
3. "The New Athens," *Columbian* 1: 18 (February 1943), 1.
4. Don Elton Smith, interview with author, July 16, 2007, Loveland, Colo.
5. "Why the Change?" *Columbian* 1: 18 (February 1943).
6. Eisan, *Pathways of Peace,* 408.
7. Harold Row to Mark Schrock, February 2, 1943. Davis-Kovac.
8. Letters exchanged by Charles Davis and Eleanor Ring, January 1943. Davis-Kovac.
9. Charlie Davis to CPS #21, May 17, 1943. Davis-Kovac.
10. Charlie Davis to CPS #21, May 19, 1943. Davis-Kovac.
11. Charlie Davis to CPS #21, May 21, 1943. Davis-Kovac. The issue of pay in CPS continued even after the war, see Steve Nolt, "The CPS Frozen Fund: The Beginning of Peace-Time Interaction Between Historic Peace Churches and the United States Government," *The Mennonite Quarterly Review* 47 (1993), 201-224.
12. Charlie Davis to CPS #21, June 2, 1943. Davis-Kovac.
13. Charlie Davis to Paul French, June 18, 1943. Davis-Kovac.
14. Mark Schrock to Harold Row, January 5, 1943. Brethren. Copy in Davis-Kovac.
15. "New Committees," *Columbian* 1: 18 (February 1943), 4.
16. Harold Row to Mark Schrock, February 9, 1943. Davis-Kovac.
17. General Report on Educational Activities in CPS #21 for the months November 1944-February 1945 inclusive. Brethren. Copy in Davis-Kovac.
18. Letter to the author from Vic Langford, May 7, 2007. Davis-Kovac.
19. Memo from Harold Row to Camp Directors and CPS Men, June 2, 1943. Bridgewater. Davis-Kovac.
20. Dasenbrock, *To the Beat of a Different Drummer,* 67-68.
21. Eisan, *Pathways of Peace,* 317-321.
22. Dasenbrock, *To the Beat of a Different Drummer,* 69.
23. Robinson, "Civilian Public Service during World War II," 200-210.
24. Memo from Harold Row to Camp Directors and Unit Leaders of Hospitals, July 1, 1943. Bridgewater. Copy in Davis-Kovac.
25. Dwight Hanawalt to the author, February 3, 2007. Davis-Kovac.
26. *Illiterati 1,* 1.
27. *Illiterati 1,* last page.
28. *Illiterati 2,* 1.
29. Barber and Jones, "The Utmost Human Consequence," 510-535.
30. Kermit Sheets to unknown correspondent(s), undated, but probably written on October 21, 1942. LC Sheets.
31. Krmtt Zhiitsh, "Stalingrad Stalemate."
32. Ibid., 3.

33. Sheets to unknown correspondent(s), probably October 21, 1942. LC Sheets.

34. *Illiterati 2.*

35. For additional information about the life and career of Kermit Sheets, see internet resource, "Footprints of Pacifism: The Creative Lives of Kermit Sheets and Kemper Nomland."

36. Ibid.

37. Kermit Sheets to Morris Keeton, October 5, 1943. LC Sheets. Copy in Davis-Kovac.

38. Morris Keeton to Dick Mills and Mark Schrock, October 30, 1943. Brethren. Copy in Davis-Kovac.

39. William Everson, *The Fine Arts at Waldport*. Davis-Kovac.

40. Merchant and Skinner, *Glen Coffield, William Everson, & Publishing at Waldport, Oregon.*

41. *Printing at Waldport: William Everson, Adrian Wilson and the Legacy of the Untide Press.*

42. www.connectotel.com/marcus/pocketph.html (accessed September 7, 2007).

43. http://www.lib.uiowa.edu/exhibits/friends/wilson.html (accessed September 7, 2007); Wilson, *Two Against the Tide.*

44. "The Fine Arts at Waldport," *Compass* II: 1&2 (Fall 1944), Waldport, Oregon.

45. Letter from Mark Schrock to Harold Row, August 2, 1943, Brethren. Copy in Davis-Kovac. Unfortunately, the letter from Case to West has not yet been found.

46. Memo from Harold Row to men in Brethren CPS, August 12, 1942, Brethren. Copy in Davis-Kovac.

47. Dasenbrock, *To the Beat of a Different Drummer*, 74-78.

48. Minutes of the School of Pacifist Living, November 19, 1943. Davis-Kovac.

49. "The First Month," Memo from Dan West to school members and other interested persons, December 1943. Davis-Kovac.

50. Yoder, *Passing on the Gift: The Story of Dan West.*

51. For further information on the history and current work of Heifer International see http://www.heifer.org/ (accessed September 7, 2007).

52. Glee Yoder, *Passing on the Gift*, 64.

53. Interim reports from units 2, 5, 6, 9, and 10 were found in the various archives, but no final reports from the individual groups or from the entire school seem to have been written. All these documents are in Davis-Kovac.

54. Obituary notice for G. Bernhard Fedde. Davis-Kovac.

55. Dan West, "An Evaluation of the School of Pacifist Living. Points mentioned once or more by 15 members," March 30, 1944, and "Evaluation of the School of Pacifist Living," March 31, 1944. Brethren. Dan West Files, Box 27, Folder 41.

56. Smith, *Six Year Passage.*

57. Don Elton Smith to the author, September 11, 2006. Davis-Kovac.

58. Richard Anderson to the author, October 12, 2006. Davis-Kovac.

59. Mark Schrock to Lew Ayres, April 22, 1943. Davis/Kovac.

60. Charles Davis, interview with Dave Wershkul, about 1995. DVD copy of VHS tape in Davis-Kovac.

61. Minutes of Staff Meeting, August 13, 1942. Brethren. Copy in Davis-Kovac.

62. "Statement of Philip Isely in Federal District Court, Portland, Oregon, May 10, 1943." LC Sheets. Copy in Davis-Kovac.

63. William G. Webb, "Why I refused to work in CPS camp." LC Sheets. Copy in Davis-Kovac.

64. Charles D. Hornig to General Lewis B. Hershey, April 10, 1943. LC Sheets. Copy in Davis-Kovac.

65. Alan McRae statement, December 10, 1943. Davis-Kovac.

66. Robert McLane statement, April 10, 1944. I am indebted to the family of Robert McLane for providing me with this document. Davis-Kovac.

67. Sibley and Jacob, *Conscription of Conscience*, 337.

Chapter Seven

1. Smith, *Six Year Passage*, 30.

2. Ibid., 30-31; Newsletter for February 3, 1945. Brethren. Copy in Davis-Kovac.

3. General Report on Educational Activities in CPS #21 for the months November 1944-February 1945 inclusive. Brethren. Copy in Davis-Kovac.

4. Robinson, "Civilian Public Service during World War II," 225-227.

5. The details of the Japanese balloon bomb project were derived from the following sources: McPhee, "Balloons of War;" Prioli, "The Fu-Go Project;" "Fire Balloon," Wikipedia; Rogers, "How Geologists Unraveled the Mystery of the Japanese Vengeance Balloon Bombs in World War II."

6. Smith, *Six Year Passage*, 27-28.

7. James Townsend, Newsletter for August 15, 1945. Brethren. Copy in Davis-Kovac.

8. James Townsend, Newsletter for August 15, 1945. Brethren. Copy in Davis-Kovac.

9. Smith, *Six Year Passage*; Don Smith and Lyle Jones, undated appeal to the camp; Dave Lindsay, "Report of #21 Relief Activity, April 17, 1946." Brethren. Davis-Kovac.

10. Newsletter of October 31, 1945. Brethren. Copy in Davis-Kovac.

11. Robinson, "Civilian Public Service during World War II," chapter 9.

12. Charles Davis video interview with Dave Wershkul.

13. Smith, *Six Year Passage*, p 39. Davis-Kovac.

14. Professor Robert Gorsch of St. Mary's College kindly collected recollections from several former students and colleagues of Jim Townsend: Robert Haas, former student and currently Professor of English at the University of California, Berkeley, Brother William Beattie, former academic vice president of St. Mary's, Brother Mel Anderson, former president, and Brother Ronald Gallagher, current president of the college. These recollections are in Davis-Kovac.

15. Howard Hamilton to Harold Row and Ora Houston, August 3, 1946, on exit from Camp Cascade Locks. Brethren. Copy in Davis-Kovac.

16. Don Smith, CPS #21 Newsletter, January 25, 1946. Brethren. Copy in Davis-Kovac.

17. Robinson, "Civilian Public Service during World War II," 473.

18. Smith, *Six Year Passage*, 43.

19. Program for *The Seagull*. Davis-Kovac.

20. Broadus Erle, http://computertutorinc.net/SW-AboutBroadusErle.htm (accessed January 20, 2008).

21. Photographs from *The Seagull* February 24, 1946 are at LC Blocher.

22. Harry Prochaska, "History of CPS #21: Art Activities in CPS #21," March 1946. Davis-Kovac.

23. Mitchell L. Robinson, "Civilian Public Service during World War II," 479-485.
24. Memo #116 from Harold W. Row, June 4, 1946. Bridgewater. Copy in Davis-Kovac.
25. Howard Hamilton to Harold Row and Ora Houston, August 3, 1946. Brethren. Copy in Davis-Kovac.

Chapter Eight

1. Mark Schrock to M. R. Zigler, September 24, 1941. Brethren. Copy in Davis-Kovac.
2. Richard Anderson to the author, July 24, 2006. Davis-Kovac.
3. David Orser, CPS #21 History "Some Men of #21," 64. Davis-Kovac.
4. Smith, *Six Year Passage*, 57.
5. Marchant, *Another World Instead*, xx.
6. Bess, *Choices Under Fire*.
7. http://www.ajmuste.org/ (accessed December 17, 2008).

BIBLIOGRAPHY

Documentary Sources

Original documents used in this study were obtained from the following sources: Brethren Historical Library and Archives; Special Collections, Aubrey R. Watzek Library, Lewis & Clark College; Special Collections, Alexander Mack Library, Bridgewater College.

The following people generously contributed copies of original documents and privately published works in their possession: Don Baker, Charles Davis, Eleanor Davis, Robert McLane, Julian Schrock, Don Elton Smith.

Copies of all original documents obtained from the various archives and individuals and letters to the author cited in this book are now in the Charles Davis-Jeffrey Kovac Collection (Davis-Kovac) which will be deposited in Special Collections at Lewis & Clark College.

Interviews

Personal interviews were conducted with the following men who spent time at CPS #21: Don Baker (San Francisco, California), Harland Gibson (Sacramento, California), Joe Gunterman (Sacramento, California), Wendell Harmon (by telephone), Don Elton Smith (Loveland, Colorado), Douglas C. Strain (Portland, Oregon). Mae Henderson, widow of Bill Henderson, was also interviewed by telephone.

There are two collections of interviews with CPS #21 men and their families. One series was filmed by Norm Smith at the 1984 Reunion at the Menucha Conference Center in Corbett, Oregon, and at other locations. There are twelve videotapes. These tapes are in the possession of the author courtesy of Harold Bock. A second series was filmed by Dave Wershkul. These films have been transferred to DVD and are in the possession of the author. Both series will be archived in the Davis-Kovac Collection.

Unpublished Manuscripts

Smith, Don Elton, *Six Year Passage,* privately published, 1994. Davis-Kovac.

Schrock, Julian, *At Cascade Locks, 1940-1944,* privately published, 2005. Davis-Kovac.

CPS Publications

The Columbian (Cascade Locks [Wyeth], Oregon), 1:1 (January, 1942) to 1:18 (February 1943).

The Compass, ed. Martin Ponch. Volume 2 (three issues), Waldport, Oregon, Summer 1944 to Spring 1946.

The Illiterati 1, Wyeth, Oregon, Spring 1943 and *The Illiterati 2,* Summer 1943.

William Everson, "The Fine Arts at Waldport," Waldport, Oregon, February 1943.

The Larch Mountaineer, Cascade Locks [Wyeth], Oregon, July to August 1942 (two issues).

Kermit Sheets, "The Mikado in CPS," Waldport, Oregon: The Illiterati, 1945.

Krmtt Zhiitsh, "Stalingrad Stalemate," Wyeth, Oregon: The Illiterati, 1943.

Books

Anderson, Richard C., *Peace Was In Their Hearts,* Watsonville, CA: Correlan Publications, 1994.

Ayres, Lew, *Altars of the East,* Garden City, NY: Doubleday, 1956.

Bess, Michael, *Choices Under Fire: Moral Dimensions of World War II,* New York: Alfred A. Knopf, 2006.

Bowman, Carl F., *Brethren Society : The Cultural Transformation of a "Peculiar People",* Baltimore: Johns Hopkins University Press, 1995.

Brock, Peter and Nigel Young, *Pacifism in the Twentieth Century,* Syracuse: Syracuse University Press, 1999.

Cooney, Robert and Helen Michalowski, eds., *The Power of the People: Active Nonviolence in the United States,* Culver City, CA: Peace Press, 1977.

Daniels, Roger, *Prisoners Without Trial: Japanese-Americans in World War II,* rev. ed., New York: Hill and Wang, 2004.

Dasenbrock, J. Henry, *To the Beat of a Different Drummer,* Winona, MN: Northland Press of Winona, 1989.

deNevers, Klancy Clark, *The Colonel and the Pacifist: Karl Bendetsen-Perry Saito and the Incarceration of Japanese Americans during World War II,* Salt Lake City: University of Utah Press, 2004.

Durnbaugh, Donald F., *Pragmatic Prophet: The Life of Michael Robert Zigler,* Elgin, IL: Brethren Press, 1989.

Eisan, Leslie, *Pathways of Peace,* Elgin, IL: Brethren Publishing House, 1948.

Eller, Cynthia, *Conscientious Objectors and the Second World War,* New York; Praeger, 1991.

Frazier, Heather T. and John O'Sullivan, *We Have Just Begun to Not Fight,* New York: Twayne Publishers, 1996.

Gara, Larry and Lenna Mae, eds., *A Few Small Candles: War Resisters of World War II Tell Their Stories,* Kent, OH and London: Kent State University Press, 1999.

Gingerich, Melvin, *Service for Peace,* Akron, PA: Mennonite Central Committee, 1949.

Goossen, Rachel Waltner, *Women Against the Good War: Conscientious Objection and Gender on the American Home Front, 1941-47.* University of North Carolina Press, Gender and Culture Series, 1997.

Harmon, Wendell E., ed., *They Also Serve*, Nappanee, IN: Relief and Service Committee and the Board for Young People's Work of the Brethren in Christ Church, 1947.

Heisey, M. J., *Peace Persistence: Tracing the Brethren in Christ Peace Witness through Three Generations,* Kent, OH: Kent State University Press, 2003.

Homan, Gerlof D., *American Mennonites and the Great War: 1914-1918,* Waterloo, Ontario and Scottdale, PA: Herald Press, 1994.

Hurwitz, D. and Craig Simpson, eds., *Against the Tide: Pacifist Resistance in the Second World War, An Oral History,* New York: War Resisters League, 1984.

Irons, Peter, *Justice at War: The Story of the Japanese-American Internment Cases,* New York and Oxford: Oxford University Press, 1983.

Keegan, John, *The Second World War,* New York: Penguin Books, 1990.

Keegan, John, *A History of Warfare.* New York: Alfred A. Knopf, 1993.

Keim, Albert N., *The CPS Story: An Illustrated History of Civilian Public Service,* Intercourse, PA: Good Books, 1969.

Keim, Albert N. and Grant M. Stoltzfus, *The Politics of Conscience: The Historic Peace Churches and America at War, 1917-1955,* Scottdale, PA, and Kitchener, Ontario: Herald Press, 1988.

Kennedy, David M., *Freedom From Fear: The American People in Depression and War, 1929-1945,* New York and Oxford: Oxford University Press, 2005.

Kraybill, Donald B. and Carl F. Bowman, *On the Backroad to Heaven: Old Order Hutterites, Mennonites, Amish, and Brethren,* Baltimore and London: Johns Hopkins University Press, 2001.

Lee, Marshall M., *A Passion for Quality: The First Fifty-five Years of Electro Scientific Industries, 1944-1999,* Portland, OR: Electro Scientific Industries, 1999.

Marchant, Fred, ed., *Another World Instead: The Early Poems of William Stafford, 1937-1947,* St. Paul, MN: Graywolf Press, 2008.

Matthews, Mark, *Smoke Jumping on the Western Fire Line,* Norman: University of Oklahoma Press, 2006.

NIBSCO, *1996 Directory of Civilian Public Service,* Washington, DC: NSBCO, 1996.

Nunnaly, Joe, *I Was a Conscientious Objector,* Berkeley, CA: Sooner Publishing Co., 1948.

Saryan, Alex, *The Turning Point,* Washington, DC: American Psychiatric Press, 2005.

Sibley, Mulford Q. and Philip E. Jacob, *Conscription of Conscience,* Ithaca, NY: Cornell University Press, 1952.

Stafford, William, *Down in My Heart,* Corvallis, OR: Oregon State University Press, 2006 reprint of the 1947 edition published by Brethren Press, Elgin, IL.

tenBroek, Jacobus, Edward N. Barnhart and Floyd W. Matson, *Prejudice, War and the Constitution,* Berkeley and Los Angeles: University of California Press, 1954.

Tracy, James, *Direct Action: Radical Pacifism from the Union Eight to the Chicago Seven,* Chicago and London: University of Chicago Press, 1996.

Tucker, Todd, *The Great Starvation Experiment,* New York: Free Press, 2006.

Wilson, Adrian (Joyce Lancaster Wilson, ed), *Two Against the Tide: A Conscientious Objector in World War II, Selected Letters 1941-1948,* Austin, TX: W. Thomas Taylor, 1990.

Wilson, Robert E., *Aideen MacLennon: The Story of a Rebel,* New York: Fellowship Publications, 1952.

Wittner, Lawrence S., *Rebels Against War: The American Peace Movement, 1941-1960*, New York and London: Columbia University Press, 1969.

Yoder, Glee, *Passing on the Gift: The Story of Dan West*, Elgin, IL: Brethren Press, 1978.

Zahn, Gordon C., *Another Side of War: The Camp Simon Story*, Amherst, MA: The University of Massachusetts Press, 1979.

Dissertations, Theses and Senior Essays

Bowman, Rufus David, "An Historical and Interpretive Study of the Church of the Brethren and War," Ph.D. Dissertation, Northwestern University, 1944.

Grimsrud, Theodore G., "An Ethical Analysis of Conscientious Objection to World War II," Ph.D. dissertation, Graduate Theological Union, 1988.

Lemke, Gretchen J., "World War II Radical Pacifists: Wartime Experience and Postwar Activism," M.A. Thesis, San Francisco State University, 1988.

Robinson, Mitchell L., "Civilian Public Service during World War II: The Dilemmas of Conscience and Conscription in a Free Society," Ph.D. dissertation, Cornell University, 1990.

Wachs, Theodore R., "Conscription, Conscientious Objection, and the Context of American Pacifism, 1940-1945," Ph.D. dissertation, University of Illinois, 1976.

Wallach, Glenn, "The CO Link: Conscientious Objection to World War II and the San Francisco Renaissance," Senior Essay, Yale University, 1981.

Articles and Book Chapters

Barber, Katrine and Eliza Elkins Jones, "The Utmost Human Consequence," *Oregon Historical Quarterly* 107: 4 (2006), 510-535.

Dahlke, H. Otto, "Values and Group Behavior in Two Camps for Conscientious Objectors," *American Journal of Sociology* 51(1) (1945), 22-33.

Davis, Charles, "Attorney for the Betrayed," *Oregon State Bar Bulletin* 59 (8) (June 1999), 15-18.

Davis, Charles, "Land of the Free?" *Oregon State Bar Bulletin* 59 (9) (July 1999), 19-24.

Davis, Charles and Jeffrey Kovac, "Confrontation at the Locks: A Protest of the Japanese Removal and Incarceration," *Oregon Historical Quarterly* 107: 4 (2006), 486-509.

Dekar, Paul R., "The "Good War" and Baptists Who Refused to Fight It," *Peace and Change* 32:2 (2007), 186-202.

Eisenberg, Ellen, "'As Truly American as Your Son': Voicing Opposition to Interment in Three West Coast Cities," *Oregon Historical Quarterly* 104: 4 (2004), 542-65.

Frost, Jennifer, "Conscientious Objection and Popular Culture: The Case of Lew Ayres," in *Challenge to Mars: Essays on Pacifism from 1918 to 1945*, edited by Peter Brock and Thomas P. Socknat, Toronto: University of Toronto Press, 1999.

McPhee, John, "Balloons of War," *New Yorker*, Jan 29, 1960, 52-60.

Nolt, Steve, "The CPS Frozen Fund: The Beginning of Peace-Time Interaction Between Historic Peace Churches and the United States Government, *The Mennonite Quarterly Review* 47 (1993), 201-224.

Orser, Edward, "Involuntary Community: Conscientious Objectors at Patapsco State Park During World War II," *Maryland Historical Magazine* 72 (1997), 132-146.

Orser, Edward, "World War II and the Pacifist Controversy in the Major Protestant Churches," *American Studies* 14: 2 (1973), 5-24.

Prioli, Carmine A., "The Fu-Go Project," *American Heritage* 33: 4 (April/
May 1982), http://www.americanheritage.com/articles/magazine/
ah/1982/3/1982_3_88.shtml, (accessed October 3, 2007).

Rise, Eric W., Review of *The Case of Odell Waller and Virginia Justice, 1940-1942,* by
Richard B. Sherman, *Journal of Southern History* 60 (1994), 167-8.

Stewart-Winter, Timothy, "Not a Soldier, Not a Slacker: Conscientious Objectors
and Male Citizenship in the United States during the Second World War,"
Gender and History 19: 3 (2007), 519-541.

Internet Resources

"About Morris Keeton." http://www.umuc.edu/odell/irahe/morris.html
(accessed 2/8/07).

"Camp 56: An Oral History Project, World War II Conscientious Objectors and the
Waldport, Oregon Civilian Public Service Camp." http://www.ccrh.org/oral/
co.pdf (accessed November 13, 2007).

"The CO Project." http://speak4peace.com/thecoproject.html (accessed
November 13, 2007).

"Fire Balloon." Wikipedia, http://en.wikipedia.org/wiki/Fire_balloon (accessed,
October 3, 2007);

"Footprints of Pacifism: The Creative Lives of Kemper Nomland and
Kermit Sheets." http://digitalcollections.lclark.edu/cgibin/showfile.
exe?CISOROOT=/pubs&CISOPTR=41 (accessed November 14, 2007)

"The Good War and Those Who Refused to Fight It." http://www.pbs.org/itvs/
thegoodwar/ (accessed, March 13, 2008).

Merchant, Paul and Jeremy Skinner, *Glen Coffield, William Everson, & Publishing
at Waldport, Oregon.* http://digitalcollections.lclark.edu/cdm4/item_viewer.
php?CISOROOT=/pubs&CISOPTR=22&CISOBOX=1&REC=1 (accessed
October 9, 2008).

*Printing at Waldport: William Everson, Adrian Wilson and the Legacy of the Untide
Press* http://digitalcollections.lclark.edu/cgi-bin/showfile.exe?CISOROOT=/
pubs&CISOPTR=16&filename=17.pdf (accessed September 7, 2007).

Rogers, J. D. "How Geologists Unraveled the Mystery of the Japanese Vengeance
Balloon Bombs in World War II," http://web.umr.edu/~rogersda/forensic_
geology/Japanese%20vengenance%20bombs%20new.htm, (accessed October
3, 2007).

Index